MILTON'S PROSODY

MILTON'S PROSODY

with a chapter on

Accentual Verse

Notes

by

ROBERT BRIDGES

OXFORD

AT THE CLARENDON PRESS

Oxford University Press, Ely House, London W. 1
GLASGOW NEW YORK TORONTO MELBOURNE WELLINGTON
CAPE TOWN SALISBURY IBADAN NAIROBI LUSAKA ADDIS ABABA
BOMBAY CALCUTTA MADRAS KARACHI LAHORE DACCA
KUALA LUMPUR HONG KONG TOKYO

FIRST PUBLISHED 1921
REPRINTED LITHOGRAPHICALLY IN GREAT BRITAIN
AT THE UNIVERSITY PRESS, OXFORD
FROM SHEETS OF THE FIRST EDITION
1965, 1967

PREFACE

WHEN I had finished the revise of this book, and in some parts rewritten it, the need of a preface confronted me, and, feeling disinclined to write anything, I fell to considering prefaces in general, and I thought of that great treatise-maker, Cicero, who, if I truly remember, kept a store of prefaces on hand, so that when he had perfected any dissertation, he had but to select from his stock the accomplished little lucubration that appeared most suitable, or, as we should say, the one that would *do best.* But even had this elegant method wholly pleased me, I had no prefaces ready on hand : and then I saw what a thousand pities it is that a book cannot write its own preface. One imagines the growing book as its organization develops and gradually gathers into unifying existence, bursting at completion into personal self-consciousness, opening like the flower of a child's mind to the miracle of its being ; then I fancied how it would come slowly to muse on its creation, to feel the discomforts inseparable from mortal existence, till it arose in the rebellion of artistic dissatisfaction to be critical of its creator. Few indeed are the books which, like the children of the wise woman, would rise up and bless their parent : they would talk rather like those who with preposterous intelligence grumble at their fate, complaining that their brains are too dependent on their stomachs, or that their knee-joints are clumsily fashioned, and their toes unsightly and useless; they might even emulate the bold proficiency of the German Helmholtz who asserted that, if he the creature had only been the Creator, he would have supplied mankind with a better eye.

Then I took sorrowful compassion on my deaf and dumb child, a poor little grammar, not born to be clothed in gorgeous raiment of morocco or enamelled leather, to lie golden-edged on drawing-room tables or by the king's bedside; yet surely with some honest faculty of delicate feeling and, alas! all the inconveniences of an embryonic and embarrassed inheritance, pains like to those which we ourselves—whether from bestial ancestry or a fall from Paradise—know too well, our

> Dropsies and asthmas and joint-racking rheums,

with all other ills that flesh is heir to: and with these pitiable imperfections of body it would bewail its ignorance, the frailties and baulking limitations of its reasoning powers, and be deeply troubled at soul by unintelligible glimpses of spiritual beauty, those adumbrations of glory, those interrupted strains and broken echoes of poetry, those flashes of Miltonic music that are embedded in it without consequence or correlation.

I wish, indeed, that it could relieve itself by utterance of vituperation against me its maker. I should rejoice, not only because my sense of justice and sport would welcome it—nor would I resent unpleasant truths—but because such a prelude would be attractive and useful to my readers, and supply that first utility of a preface, which is to spare critics the labour of examining the book. This cannot be. One service, however, I can render better than the book itself could have done it; I can tell the story of its creation: but as that is not fit for a preface I shall put it among the notes at the end.

CONTENTS

PART I

PART II

PART III

PART IV

PART I

ON THE PROSODY OF

PARADISE LOST

In this treatise the scheme adopted for the examination of Milton's matured prosody in the blank verse of *Paradise Lost* is to assume a normal regular line, and tabulate all the variations as exceptions to that norm.

Method.

For this purpose English blank verse may conveniently be regarded as a decasyllabic line on a disyllabic basis and in rising rhythm (i.e. with accents or stresses on the alternate even syllables); and the disyllabic units may be called *feet*.

Let such lines as the following be taken as normal lines,[1]

> Of thát Forbídden Trée, whose mórtal tást. i. 2.
> Torménts him; roúnd he thrǿws his báleful éyes. 56.
> A Fórrest húge of Speárs: and thrónging Hélms, 547.

and we find that these lines have ten syllables with five stresses all on the even places.

In the following chapters we will examine the exceptions to these conditions, namely:

I Exceptions to the number of syllables being ten,
II Exceptions to the number of stresses being five,
III Exceptions in the position of the stresses,

and this will give all the variations due to prosody; for quantity, though a main factor of rhythm, is not considered in the prosody of syllabic verse.

Consideration of quantity excluded.

[1] In accentual blank verse these would be normal lines, see p. 38; but the rhythmical basis of syllabic blank verse has never been satisfactorily determined, nor will it be discussed in this book; see ch. II, pp. 37 and 38, and again on p. 84.

[§ Digression on Quantity.

What quantity is.

Quantity, which means the relative duration of time which different syllables fill in pronouncing, is an omnipresent efficient factor of rhythm, and as we are not going to deal with it, we shall do well to exhibit exactly what it is that we are excluding.

Take the first of these regular lines quoted above,

(1) Of thát | Forbíd|den Trée, | whose mór|tal tást :

this line may be read extremely well with all its five accents at perfectly regular intervals of time : Let it be so read.

If this reading be now set out in musical notation, with the isochronous musical bars (as is necessary) before the accents, we shall not get

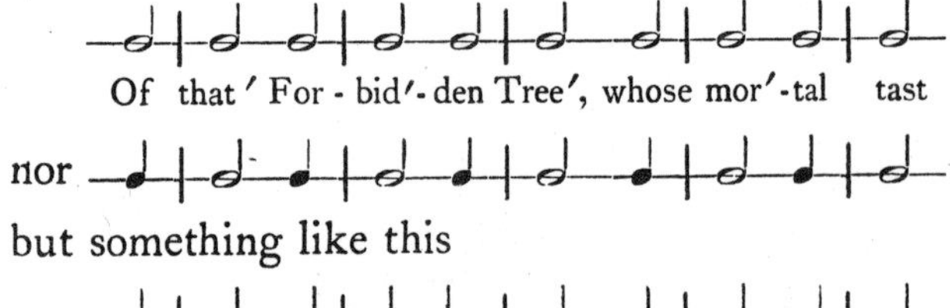

but something like this

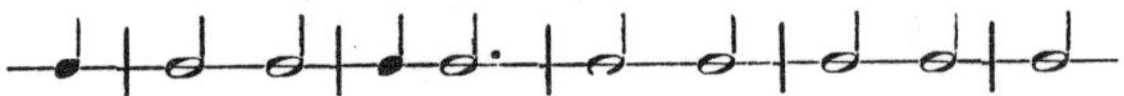

that is to say the accent in the second foot *forbid* is on a very short syllable *bid*, and the unaccented syllable *den* is held on to fill the bar : and this affects the rhythm very deeply, but it does not concern the prosody ; that is to say, the prosody admits of either long or short syllables in any place of the verse. If now we were to try to write this same line in equal-timed prosodial feet we should get

No quantitive rule for the feet in English syllabic verse.

Of that | Forbid'n͡|n Tree, whose mor-tal tast :

and although one very effective and common way of reciting the verse of *P. L.* is to set up an equal-timed musical beat and keep as nearly to it as possible, yet such a reading will sometimes give five and sometimes only four bars to the verse; and if it serve for a *rhythmical* interpretation, it will exhibit to the ear, as the notation above exhibits to the eye, the fact that time-value or quantity is not considered in the prosody of English syllabic verse any more than classical prosody concerns itself with the rhythms produced by the incidence of the verbal accents on the prescribed prosodial units, although in each case these rhythms are primal factors in the beauty of the verse.

Common confusion of accent and quantity.

The example of the word *forbidden* will show what it is that English writers on metre confuse, when they call accented syllables 'long', and take all unaccented syllables to be 'short'.

That in syllabic English verse the *prosody proper* is not concerned with the rhythmical effects caused by 'quantity' (i.e. by the different lengths of the syllables when spoken) may possibly give rise to the idea that there is no such thing as 'quantity' in English speech: and if a man can persuade himself that he is insensible to the actual different time-length of spoken syllables—as roughly illustrated above—he may possibly consider himself at liberty to apply the terms 'long' and 'short' to accented and unaccented syllables as such. The confusion is of course irremediable; and it is little credit to such exponents of verse that, having deprived these essential terms of their proper meaning, they do not, when they discuss rhythm, seem hampered in their vocabulary by the absence of any terms that distinguish these primary and omnipresent conditions.

To clinch the absurdity, note the indisputable fact that they cannot speak without differentiation of the quantities of the syllables, but yet they maintain that they cannot differentiate them. It is fruitless to show colours to the blind.

One typical example.

One example may be of use. The Greek word τετυμμένος is in quantity and accent similar to such

English words as *scientific*, *apostolic*, *unemphatic*, *disembody*, *recognition*, *unambitious*, *anaesthetic*, &c., and may be represented in musical notation thus,

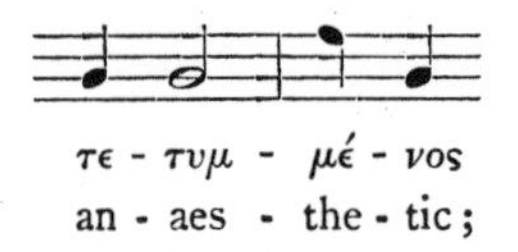

but boys are taught to accent the Greek word as if it were Latin, and the Latin rule being that short penultimates are unaccented and in polysyllables throw the accent back, they pronounce the word thus :

in doing this the long unaccented syllable τυμμ (with its double μ) is *shortened by being accented*, because the μμ is treated as if it were merely the English device of marking the short quality of a preceding accented vowel, instead of giving syllabic length by the production of the liquid μ. Both accent and quantity are thus falsified, the long syllable is pronounced short, and the accented syllable is unaccented; and thus it is that boys are expensively trained to be incapable of distinguishing between accent and quantity, and to read all Greek and Latin verse wrongly.]

I. *Exceptions to the syllables being ten.*

These exceptions may be either of deficiency or excess.

ℂ Deficiency of syllables.

Nine-syllable line.

There is no example in *P. L.* of a line having less than ten syllables ; but this is worth noting because it is probable that Milton was acquainted with Chaucer's practice of using a line that omits the first unaccented syllable, as in these examples from his most perfected style in the Prologue to the Tales:

> Ginglen in a whistling wind as clere. 170.
> For to delen with no swich poraille. 247.
> Twenty bokes, clad in blak or reed. 294.

and one cannot read Chaucer unless one is prepared for this. It must be concluded that Milton rejected this form of the line, though the question may be raised again in considering the rhythms in *Samson Agonistes*. In the first edition of *P. L.* there happened to be a nine-syllable line printed at x. 827,

> With me; how can they acquitted stand;

this was corrected in the 1674 edition thus,

> With me; how can they then acquitted stand.
> (Beeching, p. 401.)

¶ Supernumerary syllables.

These should be separated into two classes. First, those which may be considered as Extrametrical; secondly, those that are to be accounted for by Poetical Elision and speech contraction. And first to define the extrametrical.

§ Extrametrical syllables.

1. At end of the line.

Final extra-metrical

An extra syllable sometimes occurs at the end of the line, more rarely in Milton than in most writers, e.g.

> Of Rebel Angels, by whose aid aspiring. i. 38.

sometimes there are two such syllables.

> Imbu'd, bring to thir sweetness no satietie. viii. 216.
> For solitude somtimes is best societie. ix. 249. *P.R.* i. 302.

It is possible that these words *satiety* and *society* are allowed in this place because they admit of 'elision' [see below] and can be therefore considered as single 'hangers': but the elision being optional—(compare the following lines

What higher in her | soci|etie | thou findst. viii. 586.
Him with her lov'd | soci|etie, | that now. ix. 1007.
In solemn troops, and sweet | soci|eties. *Lyc.* 179.)—

all such endings, having two syllables extrametrical at the end, whether theoretically elidible or not, will still have a hexametric effect, and they do not differ from verses intended to have six feet. This ambiguity of prosody is illustrated in *Sam. Ag.* see p. 61. The matter worth noticing is that Milton is sparing in the use of all such endings in blank verse. (See note B).

Mid-verse extra-metrical

2. In other parts of the line.

In Shakespeare it is common to find an analogous syllable in the midst of the line; and thus Milton, in his earlier work, e.g. in *Comus*,

To quench the drouth of Phoe(bus), which as they taste. l. 66.
And as I past, I wor(shipt): if those you seek. 302.
And earths base built on stub-(ble). But com let's on. 599.
But for that damn'd magi-(cian), let him be girt. 602.
Root-bound, that fled Apol-(lo). Fool do not boast. 662.
Cramms, and blasphemes his fee-(der). Shall I go on? 779.

In *P. L.* Milton disallowed the use of this syllable. In lines like the following,

Of high collateral glor(ie): him Thrones and Powers. x. 86.

where its rhythmical effect is maintained by the colon, the extra syllable is accounted for by 'elision'.

[§ Digression on the midverse extrametrical syllable.

its French origin.

I suppose there is no doubt that this midverse extrametrical syllable came from the old French practice of regarding their twelve-syllable line as composed of two hemistichs divided by a marked caesura: concerning which Littré writes in the preface to his translation of the first book of the *Iliad*:

'Autrefois l'hémistiche était considéré comme une fin de vers. Ainsi dans un poème du XIIe siècle il est dit de Berthe:

Oncque plus douce chose ni vi, ne n'acointrai ;
Elle est plus gracieuse que n'est la rose en mai.

in twelve-syllable verse.

Et . . . d'un guerrier blessé à mort :

Pinabaux trebucha sur l'herbe ensanglantée
Et fors de son poing destre lui échappa l'epée.

Cette habitude est constante ;'

but it was discarded in the seventeenth century.

in ten-syllable verse.

The practice also invaded the French ten-syllable verse, and as this has no middle it divided it unequally. There are two examples in these five lines :

Quant vient en mai que l'on dit as lons jors,
Que Franc de France repairent de roi cort,
Reynauz repaire devant el premier front ;
Si s'en passa lez lo meis Erembor,
Ainz n'en dengna le chief drecier amont.[1]

in Shakespeare.

This extrametrical syllable being originally attached to the old caesura of the twelve-syllable line, its place is properly after the sixth syllable, as in all the examples quoted from *Comus*, but the indeterminate position of the break in ten-syllable verse allowed it to appear in other places as a few quotations from Shakespeare will illustrate. After the fourth place it is common, and this corresponds with the French examples just quoted,

Burnt on the wat(er): the poop was beaten gold. *Ant. & Cle.* ii. 2.
From mine own know(ledge). As nearly as I may. Ibid.

but in *The Tempest*, his last play (?), we find

So dear the love my people bore (me),—nor set. *Temp.* i. 2.
With all the honours on my broth(er) : whereon.

This extrametrical syllable within the line is then a borrowed licence and has no title to admission into English syllabic blank verse, but Shakespeare made a very good use of it in his dialogue. Where a line is divided between two speakers, the second speaker often disregards the last syllable of the first speaker,

[1] Quoted from *Les Poëtes français*. Crepet, vol. i. p. 42. Twelfth century.

and treats it as extrametrical. This avoids the effect of the second speaker having his answer conditioned for him by the first, who being in possession of the line ceded as it were only as much as he chose ; and in drama the value of a reply is actually impaired, if it seems to be led up to and prearranged, so as to fall pat. A stichomythia, as it is called, in which each speaker is bound to fill and not to exceed one line, requires the art to be free from all realism whatever ; a condition not often presented by our drama.

The extrametrical syllable in the condition above described is so common in Shakespeare that the ear becomes familiarized with it, and does not resent it in other places : it was freely abused by the Elizabethan dramatists : it has probably become confounded with the true trisyllabic foot and imagined to be a bad attempt at that : some modern writers have thus used it, with a sort of affectation of antique robustiousness.]

its effect obtained by elision.

There is no foot in Milton's line where this effect cannot be obtained by interrupted elision, as

> Departed from (thee), and thou resembl'st now. iv. 839.
> Before (thee) ; and not repenting, this obtaine. x. 75.

and the conditions are sometimes very elaborate, e.g. in the following line the last syllable of *condescension* appears to be extrametrical, if the prosodial elision of *be honour'd* is neglected ; and as that is optional, it cannot be said that the *effect* of the extrametrical is not intended : but Milton's rules would not have allowed the line without the elision

> Thy condescension, and shall b*e* *ho*nour'd ever. viii. 649.

Had the midverse extrametrical syllable been admitted into *P. L.*, the whole prosody would have been thrown into confusion.

§ Supernumerary syllables accounted for by Elision.

[§ Digression justifying the use of the term Elision.

Since the word elision signifies 'cutting out', there would seem an impropriety in using it to describe the condition of syllabic vowels which are not truly elided or cut out of the pronunciation. The following justification of my use of it is provoked by my critics, to whom I hereby dispense the readers' maledictions.

Elision or syn-alœpha.

In English verse when there is poetic elision of the terminal vowel of one word before the initial vowel of the next word, the sound of it is not lost, the two vowels are glided together, and the conditions may be called synalœpha.

terminal elision.

For instance the first example of terminal synalœpha in *P. L.* is

> Above th' Aonian Mount, while it pursues. i. 15.

where the final vowel of *the* is glided into the A of Aonian, it is still heard in the glide, though prosodially asyllabic.

Now since this synalœpha of vowels between two words was historically an imitation of the true Greek elision, that name is convenient and historically correct, and it is commonly used by correct grammarians, and as a matter of fact the first of two such vowels is theoretically 'cut out' of the prosody or scansion.

In Milton's prosody, this terminal 'elision' is not confined to naked vowels, he treats the semivowels *l*, *n*, and *r* as vowels, so that his terminal 'elisions' require different phonetic explanations, and would not all fall under one definite grammatical name.

Moreover when these same collisions of vowels and semivowels occur (under the same phonetic conditions) within the word, he subjects them to the same prosodial law as when they are terminal, that is between two words. The various phonetic conditions are the same in both cases, and it is convenient to have one name to cover all.

came from Greek prosody.

It might be argued that the terminal synalœpha is not the type, but is itself a mere extension of the midword synalœpha native to our speech; but since historically the Chaucerian and Miltonic terminal synalœpha seems to be the true direct descendant, a great-grandchild of the Greek elision, I preferred a term which recognized that kinship; and if in our prosody all such cases of syllabic loss are to have a general term, then 'elision' is justifiable, and is the better for having no phonetic significance; it does not describe any one of the conditions, and cannot be mistaken for anything but a label.

Greek elision.

I suppose that the practice of terminal synalœpha actually came to our verse something in this way: Firstly—In Greek when a word ended with a naked vowel, then, if the following word began with a vowel, the naked terminal vowel was cut out; it was neither spoken nor written: and this was true elision.

This condition of things raises some curious questions in Greek prosody.

Coalescence of words.

Greek grammarians are, I believe, agreed that a Greek syllable was essentially and typically composed of a consonant (or consonants) followed by a vowel; and thus in all Greek manuscripts, and subsequently in print, where a word is divided between two lines, the division is made on this principle, phonetically, regardless of the philological articulation of the word. For instance, they would have divided a word like *disorderly* not *dis-orderly* as we do, but *di-sorderly*, the *s* being annexed to the second syllable, to complete it. However strange this division may look to us, we ourselves observe it in singing, and that shows it to have a phonetic propriety of some kind. We must suppose that the Greeks used the same practice in reading as they did in writing, and that e.g. Μῆνιν ἄειδε was read as Μηνι ναειδε. But a word beginning with a vowel if it were preceded by a word that ended with a vowel would have no consonant with which to initial itself except by the practice of elision, which seems to have come of an opisthophagic habit by which it ate away the final vowel of the preceding word, if that was short and syllabically unimportant, in order to get at the last consonant and annex it to complete its own first syllable. This I imagine may have been the origin of Greek elision.

The verbal unit

Now words thus treated renounce in speech their proper formal unity; and this coalesced condition would seem at first sight irreconcilable with the great importance which the Greeks attached to the verbal unit, as that plainly appears in all their laws for caesuras and verbal breaks, in their incommunicable sensibility to the effect of a trisyllable at the end of an iambic line, and their strict disallowance of unequal division of the fourth foot in the hexameter. Such rules imply that the verbal unit had to them an overruling force, and it might seem that the recognition of that was incompatible with the phonetic amalgamation of the words. I have never come across any treatment of this question: the facts, I think, show that the phonetic amalgamation of the words cannot in any way have destroyed the force of the verbal unit—which has some special recognition perhaps in the fact that elision rules between words, but not between similar syllables within words—and if that is so, we must conclude that its force did not lie in its formal literary structure, but in the voice-tone which translated it to the plane of ideas and emotions.

(in voice-tone)

I suppose that it is something of this sort. The entrance of any important word into the verse is a call of the attention by change of voice-tone to some *idea*, with its trail of associations ; and this attention implies duration ; the attention is shifted to a certain level and as it were held there until it is released by the new call of the next word ; and in the break between the two, that part of our mind which is attending to the metre is conscious of the place where it has arrived. The coarseness of such an analysis is apparent, but the subtlety and obscurity of our subconscious intelligence defy definition, and I only try to suggest the plane on which these effects are alive. If it is somewhat as I suggest, then the value of word-length is well explained, and also the advantage of recognizing enclitics and proclitics. We certainly recognize the force of the verbal unit in English, almost as much as the Greeks did, although the monosyllabic quality of our language is unfavourable to the full use of its best effects.

has no rules in English prosody.

If it should be questioned what place this discussion has here, I would point out that the rules for the position of verbal units were an essential matter in Greek prosody, but that we, though bound to recognize their almost equal force in our own verse, do not regard them as subject to laws of prosody. Milton, so far as I know, has no rule for the division of feet between words, although his practice is no doubt subtle and careful enough. In English syllabic verse the rules for the distribution of syllables as of quantities are absent.

Elision in Latin verse.

Secondly—when the Latins discarded their native accentual verse and invented their close imitation of the Greek, they adopted the same rule of excluding these naked terminal vowels from their reckoning of syllables in the scansion ; but, as their habit of speech required, they still wrote them, and did not wholly cut them out of the pronunciation, but glided the two colliding vowels together, as is done to this day in Italian verse.

Latin synalœpha inconsistent.

This gliding together of vowels, called synalœpha, being forced into the reading of Latin verse as a conscious device whereby the prosody might be assimilated to the Greek, produced what seems a gross inconsistency in the system of the Latins ; because they applied it only to the naked vowels that collided between separate words, and not to the same vowels colliding within the word : and though they followed the Greeks in this, it must in their own practice have been a distinction without a difference. And even the terminal vowels that had no true phonetic glide were forced into the synalœpha that was forbidden to the most confluent vowel-combinations within the word, such as are more easily glided together than kept syllabically independent.

On such questions of speech-condition I have not learning enough to formulate anything above a very modest opinion ; but history seems to show that our European versification has been strongly determined through the Romance languages by Latin practice ; and however that may have been adapted to suit different conditions, it may well have been the cause of logical inconsistencies : and this knowledge should forbid us to assume that the laws which at any time ruled in any school of poetry were the result of free experiment. Convention has been very strong. In versification we know that the manner to which every one is accustomed, even though it be pedantry, has a far greater propriety to our ears than that which we should rightly prefer if we were not prejudiced by custom—the ridiculous distortion of sense and speech-rhythm in the chanting of the Psalms by the trained choirs of our Cathedrals is a good example —and one can only say that the Latins trained them-

Force of convention.

selves to regard the collision of vowels between words as a different condition from the same collision within a word, and that this convention was handed down. But when French theorists argue that the laws of hiatus enforced by Malherbe are rubbish *because* the same forbidden conditions are tolerated within words, it is not thereby proved that the forbidden conditions are agreeable, or that it is not better to avoid them. Nor have they the right to *assume* that the ends of words are in the same conditions as their middles; for the word as a unit demands special treatment, and it may have been unconsciously protected by the very inconsistency that they denounce.

Romance verse

Thirdly—when the syllabic poetry of the Romance languages arose, its basis was the inheritance of the corrupted quantitive Latin practice; and we have to explain how quantitive verse became syllabic. I would here again plainly warn the reader that I have never been a serious student in this field, and that my knowledge is most superficial and fragmentary; scattered examples, however, seem to me to admit of one simple interpretation, concerning which I feel no doubt, and it would be as follows.

how it became syllabic.

The recognition of only two lengths of syllables, on which the Greek and Latin prosody had depended, though convenient and defensible, was artificial, and was bound to perish from practice in the lapse of tradition; so that the early ecclesiastical Latin verse-writers, in following the old verse-forms, while they satisfied their ear by preserving something of the old superimposed accentual rhythms—for those could not be misread—, neglected the old quantities, and merely counted the syllables as units of the feet, omitting from that reckoning the naked terminal vowels which they no doubt still glided together. Some of the old hymns look as if the tradition of observing the law of terminal elision was lost,[1] and hiatus is common in old French verse; but this rule of elision eventually survived, and the whole of Romance verse thus became syllabic and subject to the Latin elision. Eventually this terminal synalœpha was consistently extended to the collision of gliding vowels within the word in the early Italian and French verse.

Chaucer followed it.

Fourthly—when Chaucer adopted the Romance prosody he imitated the French very closely; and it was thus that the Latin practice, as handed down by the Romance writers, came into English verse.

Milton followed him.

It would be essential for a thorough treatment of the subject to give the rules which Chaucer elaborated, but unfortunately this is not possible. The difficulty of fully formulating his practice is due to his having extended it gradually, so that it is developed only in his latest writing—and this is the same with Milton—; and since his later work can in many cases be dated only by the prosody, this uncertainty together with that of the manuscripts and of the syllabic values of the French words makes it impossible to proceed without unwarrantable assumption of some of the questions in dispute. I shall therefore not attempt to describe it here; and it is more easily investigated when Milton's rules are understood, since those would appear to be only a learned systemization of Chaucer's practice.[2]

extended application.

The main point is that the elision (synalœpha) which in the Latin tradition ruled between words was now freely extended to the same syllabic conditions within the word, and that it was in every case

[1] Some examples are given below on p. 86.

[2] That Milton took Spenser for his master we have on Dryden's authority. I always guessed that Dryden must have asked Milton whether Spenser were not his model, and that Milton gladly assented in order to avoid a fruitless discussion on prosody,—a motive which I can well understand.

optional[1]; and it is no doubt a liberty in my terminology to extend the prosodial term 'elision' to cover all these conditions of syllabic loss.

Equivalence or trisyllabic feet

One reason why the historic theory of elision in English prosody is not universally recognized is that these so-called elisions may be all described as making trisyllabic feet, which are agreeable both to accentual and quantitive theorists. Moreover neither Chaucer's nor Milton's rules were ever formulated, so that their practice not being understood was not strictly observed by poets, who therefore supply apt illustrations for any theory. If the explanation of these elided syllables is quantitive they can be interpreted by the old classical rule of 'equivalence', two short syllables being equivalent to one long—as we find spondees interchangeable with dactyls, and trisyllabic feet admitted into Greek and Latin disyllabic verse. And there is no doubt that many of the elisions have this effect fully, and must have been agreeable to Milton's ear for that reason, and it is moreover evident that certain of them have their best *rhythmical* explanation on the equivalence theory. Moreover Anglo-Saxon poets had recognized 'equivalence'; at least one expert tells me that they enforced length on their accented places, so that if, in their accentual verse the accent fell on a short syllable, then that syllable needed another short syllable with it to fill up its time. Our native speech-instinct which led to this practice is, I should say, exemplified in such lines as the following in *P. L.*

re-cognized in English before Chaucer.

I had persis|ted hâppie|, had not thy pride. x. 874.
Of Éne|mie hath beguil'd thee, yet unknown. ix. 905.

[1] Optional with exception of those weak endings of words, which though they were, as experts tell us, obsolete in his day, Chaucer consistently used, being probably influenced by their similarity to French accidence, the effects of which he was imitating. Concerning the rationale of optional elision see the sections on hypermonosyllables, pp. 20 and 26.

though these verses scan by means of their elisions before *had* and *hath*, their rhythm seems to be in the equivalence, as I have divided them.

Tri-syllabic effect of synalœpha in Latin.

Although there can have been no confusion between synalœpha and true resolution by equivalence in Latin verse, yet the rhythmic effect of synalœpha must have been very plain to the ear. For instance, while Virgil's epic hexameter is much more spondaic than Homer's, his Latin lines have nearly as many syllables in them as the Greek. In Catullus's two pure iambic poems the elisions in the odd places (where spondees were normal) are twice as frequent as those in the even places. But it would be rash to deduce much from this.

in English trisyllabic verse.

Again, there is no doubt that any English poet who should write accentual trisyllabic verse (that is verse on the basis of having two unaccented syllables between the normal metric stresses), would freely use these same combinations of vowels and liquids to make his trisyllabic feet; *but he will use many other short syllables also*, and the characteristic of the Miltonic verse is that those other short syllables are forbidden to come in as couples to fill the single places of the disyllabic scheme.

Objection to equivalence theory in *P. L.*

There is one insuperable theoretic objection to explaining Milton's trisyllabic places as examples of 'equivalence' in the fact that he does not refuse to admit two classically short syllables for a full foot. On the theory of equivalence these feet are defective, so that it can be only enforced inconsistently to explain the trisyllabic places. But it matters little how these are imagined, if it be recognized that the 'equivalence' in *P. L.* is always assured by some 'elision'. Blank verse which admits into such places any kind of unaccented syllables, whether elidible or not, ceases to be syllabic verse and becomes so far accentual. There is no objection to such accentual verse, and there has been an increasing propensity to allow its forcible effects to override the subtler grace of the purely syllabic structure: and nowadays all readers of English verse are accustomed to find syllabic and accentual verses alternating in a poem; and such a poem will please them none the less; and they read the rhythms easily enough, being familiar with both manners, as the writers were, and probably enough in neither case distinguishing them. The fault of such verse is that syllabic verses coming in among accentual verses must often invite (if they do not compel) a wrong accentuation, and one cannot be forbidden to read them on the same system as one has to use for the others. The practice is artistically indefensible. It is true that the practice of optional elision brings Milton's syllabic verse under a somewhat similar objection: but its speech-rhythm gives its interpretation and leaves the prosody consistent; while in the other case it reveals the inconsistency.

As a matter then of rhythm it may well enough be maintained that Milton's elisions are trisyllabic feet; but historically and in prosody they are 'elisions', the great-grandchildren of Homeric elision.

On the extension of elision to semivowels see p. 26.

Dryden's prosody un-Miltonic.

Finally there is some indication that Dryden and his school at one time read Greek elision into Latin verse, and in their own verse intended the 'elided' vowels—which they represented by apostrophs—to be omitted from pronunciation: but if so, the absurdity perished. This anti-Miltonic school, which I should guess to have been under the influence of Malherbe, objected also to elision being optional, considering naked terminal vowels as blots on the page. Readers of Dryden and Pope are apt to acquire their un-Miltonic ear, in spite of the blots. A theory of speech which is not only unnatural but impossible to conform to, does not call for refutation. Dryden's practice is some further justification for the term 'elision'.]

§ Vowel-elisions of common speech.

Synalœpha in common speech.

In tabulating Milton's rules for poetic elision it will be convenient to separate off in a distinct class, as 'Elisions of common speech', those cases where contiguous vowels are run together in common speech, and universally recognized as making but one syllable, even though they were in earlier times separately pronounced so as to make two syllables, and still in most cases retain something of their double sound. The first line of *P.L.* gives a particularly good example,

> Of Man's First Disobedience, and the Fruit,

where the *ie* of *disobedience* is neither a diphthong nor a disyllable, and the two vowels are both heard, though they make but one syllable.

This condition came from the conversion of the first vowel into a y-glide, and the phonetic condition is exactly the same as the glide or synalœpha of the naked vowels in the poetic elision *He effected.* The difference between the two cases is this. Common speech had already adopted *obedience* as a trisyllable, and it is admitted into the verse with that value without question or option, whereas in the poetic elision a fuller pronunciation of the vowels is not only possible without archaism, but is more usual in common speech, and the synalœpha is optional.

much of it fixed about 1600.

It was in Elizabethan times that such contiguous vowels as the *ie* in *obedience* finally lost their disyllabic value: so that the syllabic values of such words is one of the most easily recognized distinctions between the earlier and later verse: and Milton in his earlier poems had used the older pronunciation, thus in Comus,

> With all the greisly legi-ons that troop. 603.
> Or gastly furies appariti-on. 641.
> By a strong siding champion Consci-ence. 212.

and thus he uses *delusi-on*, *conditi-on*, *complexi-on*, *visi-on*, *contemplati-on*, *&c.*, which were all old-fashioned and out of date: but when he wrote *P. L.* he accepted so far the pronunciation of his time, and there is no example of the old pronunciations of such words in that poem.

obsolete syllabizing still used in verse.

The usage of all poets, with regard to obsolescent pronunciations is conservative and archaic, and in our contemporary poetry it is still common to find such a word as *obedience* in full syllabic extension at the end of a line.

The line last quoted is a good example of the transitional stage, because *champion* is accepted with its *i* lost in the glide, whereas *conscience* is not.

Conscience, *patience*, *vision*, and all the host of words ending in *-ation*, are examples of words that have utterly lost the syllabic value of their *i* in the y-glide, and we are in danger now of losing the glide in these last, for our phoneticians write *-ation* as *eish'n* without any glide; but Milton respected it (p. 33).

Hyper-mono-syllables.

Vocalic.

But of words containing vowel-glides there is another intermediate class in which the words have not established absolutely fixed values in English prosody. It is not our business to treat them historically or philologically, but their prosody should be considered in this place.

The typical and common examples of the y-glide are, *fire*, *desire*, *tire*, *&c.* e.g.

> That fires the length of Ophiucus huge. ii. 709.

and of the w-glide, *our*, *hour*, *flower*, *power*, *poor*, *fewer*, *&c.*

Of these words Milton used *power* as a disyllable in *Penseroso*.

> Whose powër hath a true consent. 95.

But in *P. L.* it is always a monosyllable e.g.

> Powers and Dominions, Deities of Heav'n. ii. 11.
> His utmost power with adverse power oppos'd. i. 103.

and though *power* became recognized as monosyllabic in English poetry it has still partly maintained its right to be used as a disyllable, e.g.

Are portions of one powër, which is mine. Shelley, *Ap.* 14.
A powër from the unknown God. *Hellas*, 211.
Yet not for powër (powër of herself. Tennyson, *Œnone*.

The following examples will illustrate the uncertain value of these words.

Than tir'd (tieřd) eyelids upon tir'd eyes. Tennyson, *Lotos*.
As Desiřes lightning feet. Shelley, *Prom.* i. 734.
Thou most desired (ieřd) Hoûr, more loved and lovely. iii. 3. 69.
Upon that path where floweřs never grew. *Triumph*, 65.
Few floweřs grow upon thy wintry way. *Fragment* (p. 580).
With blackest moss the floweř-plots. Tennyson.
Higher still and higher Shelley, *Skylark*.

where the first higher is a disyllable (as elsewhere) the second rhymes with fire, which he almost always uses as a monosyllable, but

To hear the fiře roar and hiss. *Marianne's Dream*, xvii.
The lyre's (lieřs) voice is lovely everywhere. M. Arnold.

their typical phonetic condition

Let us take *power* as the type and analyse the sound. It contains three vowels and a glide, and may be represented to the eye thus, p ɑ u w ə (r), giving a strong vowel or diphthongal sound *au* followed by a weak vowel sound ə, the two being connected by a falling w-glide; nor can this be shortened: the only question that can be made is whether the u and the w are both present, or whether the place of the vowel (u) be not wholly occupied by the glide (w). But since in proportion as the sound of the long vowel is disallowed, the strength of the glide is asserted, it does not seem to matter how this is decided.

a precedent for optional elision.

There is no doubt that *power* is generally received into English verse as a monosyllable, and thus is sometimes written *pow'r* or *powr*; but the omission of the sound indicated by the apostroph is not effected by omitting it from the spelling; the word is always a strong vowel glided into a weak one, and the introduction of such units into the verse clears the way for all other 'elisions' of vowel sequences which can be treated in a like manner[1]: and if such a unit can be regarded as either monosyllabic or disyllabic at will, that is also a full precedent for such elisions being in other cases optional.

Again, when considering the semivowel elisions we shall find quite another set of hypermonosyllables, which having the same doubtful syllabic value as *power &c.* are treated by the prosody in the same way as filling either one or two places in the syllabic verse.

Apparent exceptions.

Note that the apparently similar words (which are always monosyllabic) *air fair prayer bare, &c.*, and *ear, hear, fear, &c.*, differ from the type *power*, the first in having almost no tail-glide to their accented vowel; the second set by having their accented vowel so short, that its glide is able wholly to supplant it. Thus dialectal speech sometimes prints *hear* or *here* as *hyah*, where the *y* is, I take it, intended for a consonant or short glide, not for a long vowel.

('toward.')

There may be some doubt perhaps how Milton contracted *toward* and *towards*. This word is generally monosyllabic in his verse, but there are these exceptions

Strait tówárd Heav'n my wondring Eyes I turn'd. viii. 257.
In Serpent, Inmate bad, and tówárd Eve. ix. 495.
Safe tówárds Canáän from the shoar advance. xii. 215.
Justification tówárds God, and peace. xii. 296.
Yet tówárd these thus dignifi'd, thou oft. *S. A.* 682.

The contraction which in our common speech is now *t'ward* used to be *toő'-rd*, and this is the better form; and since its probability is very much favoured by the five lines just quoted, it will be assumed in

[1] *Power* is of course an example of one class only. See on the two glides, next page.

the classification, and the word will fall under the *w* tail-glides, with optional elision.

§ Poetic elision of vowels.

Vocalic synalœpha depends on tail-glide.

When two vowel sounds come together, then if the first of the two has a tail-glide, there may be elision, i.e. the sounds may be glided together so as to make a sound which can be reckoned as one syllable in the disyllabic verse.

'Diphthongs' are included, and *h* is often considered as no letter.[1]

There are two vowels in English which have no tail-glide. They are the *a* of *father*, the broad *o* which we write *aw* (*law*). (The vowel in *air*, *Mary*, *&c.*—written as a diphthong by phoneticians εə—varies much and may be neglected here.)

The tailless vowels may of course be involved in elisions when they follow a gliding vowel, e.g. *th' Army*, *th' almighty*, *th' Air*.

He ceas'd; and th' Archangelic Power prepard. xi. 126.
With other notes then to th' Orphean Lyre. *P. L.* iii. 17.
They summ'd their Penns, and soaring th' air sublime. vii. 421.

For mere prosody, it would be sufficient to say that all other vowel sounds are subject to elision in all conditions, but in giving examples it may be as well to classify them phonetically.

The two glides.

They may be classified under their two glides, each of which will show three conditions.

The two glides are the y-glide and the u- (oo) or w-glide. We will take the y-glide first because it has already been illustrated in *obedience*, and *champion*, and *hear*. Its three conditions are these:

[1] The value of written *h* varies from complete suppression to the full force of a consonant; and it varies also with the speaker and again with its collocation in the sentence; so that the questions raised would not repay discussion. See p. 26.

1. When the first vowel sound is stressed as in *riot.*

2. When the second vowel sound is stressed as in *humiliátion.*

3. When neither vowel is stressed as in *Michael.*

In this third case it may be conceded that one of the two vowels is generally more stressed than the other, so that most cases of this class (and it is of course the same with the w-glide) might be correctly ascribed to one of the previous classes, but it is more convenient to class them separately.

The w-glide has the same three conditions viz.

4. When the first vowel is stressed as in *ruin.*

5. When the second vowel is stressed. Of this there is no example within the word, unless *fluctuats*, ix 668, may pass.

6. When neither vowel is stressed as in *virtuous.*

The y-glide.

Examples of all the six classes are here given.

1. *Saying*, *being*, *flying*, *diet*, *riot*, *giant*, *higher* (*hi'er*), *hierarch*, *violence*, *diamond*, *variety*, *Deity*, *piety.*

Half fl*yi*ng ; behoves him now boath Oare and Saile. ii. 942.
B*e i*t so, for I submit, his doom is fair. x. 769.
Is his wrauth also ? b*e i*t, man is not so. 795.

2. *Humiliation. Tiresias* iii. 36 (hardly any accent: see note C.) *Mediator* xii. 240, is confirmed by x. 60.

Therefore thy Humil*ia*tion shall exalt. iii. 313.
Timel*y i*nterposes, and her monthly round. iii. 728.
From Hell continu'd reaching th' utmost Orbe. ii. 1029.
Hypocrisie, th*e o*nly evil that walks. iii. 683.
His day, which else as th' other Hemisphere. iii. 725.
More grateful then harmonious sound to th*e e*are. viii. 606.

and thus *the air*, *the earth*, *the eye*, *the hour*, note that *the hour* has four vowels glided as one syllable, *iauer.*

3. *Michael*, *Sinai*, (but Milton may have pronounced this word as a disyllable :) *Michael* is a trisyllable sometimes in *P. L.* Examples of this class are almost all between words, because when within the word they are usually elisions of common speech :

Above th' Aonian Mount, while it pursues. i. 15.
To set himself in Glor*y a*bove his Peers. i. 39.
Strange horror seise th*ee*, *a*nd pangs unfelt before. ii. 703.
Though kept from Man and worthy to b*e a*dmir'd. ix. 746.
H*e e*ffected ; Man he made, and for him built. ix. 152.
Little infer*io*r, by m*y a*dventure hard. x. 468.
With spattering noise rejected : oft th*ey a*ssayd. x. 567.
Life in myself for ever, by th*ee I* live. iii. 244.
Forc't I absolve : all m*y e*vasions vain. x. 829.

and thus *the acclaim* : *the almighty*, *me and*, *thee and*, *the unwary*, *thĕe unblamed*. *Vitiated* x. 169, may belong here or to class 2.

The w-glide.

4. *doing*, *ruin*, *toward*, see p. 22.

N*o i*ngrateful food : and food alike those pure. v. 407.
With noises loud and r*ui*nous, to compare. ii. 921.

5. Examples within the word missing.

And rapture s*o o*ft beheld ? those heav'nly shapes. ix. 1082.
Int*o u*tter darkness, deep ingulft, his place. v. 614.
Of somthing not unseasonable t*o a*sk. viii. 201.

In another writer this line would have been intended and rightly read *unseas'*|*nable* | *to ask* ; and Milton has *unreasoning* with the *o* 'elided' : but his rule and use of adjectives in *able* decides certainly in favour of the elision here exemplified.

6. *followers*, *Siloa's*, *bellowing*, *shadowy*, *gradual*, *effluence*, *influence*, *extenuate*, *tumultuous*.

For God is als*o i*n sleep and Dreams advise. xii. 611.
Vert*ue i*n her shape how lovly, saw, and pin'd, iv. 848.
Presaging, since with sorr*ow a*nd hearts distress xii. 613.
Thou didst accept them ; wilt th*ou e*njoy the good. x. 758.
Damasco, or Marocc*o*, *o*r Trebisond. i. 584.
As Lords, a spacious World, t*o ou*r native Heaven. x. 467.

Elision through H.

H treated as non-consonantal

7. It is plain that there cannot be a true glide through a consonantal *h*. The following examples show various conditions. *Harp* seems to forbid synalœpha, see note D. *Horizon* may have its classical aspirate, it has none in Italian. *Whom* seems possible by using the *u* of *to* (*tu*) as a glide and disguising the *h*, = t*uhu*m. See p. 23, note.

For still they knew, and ought t*o ha*ve still remember'd. x. 12.
In Gems and wanton dress; to th*e Ha*rp they sung. xi. 579.
T' whom thus the Portress of Hell Gate reply'd. ii. 746.
Two onel*y who* yet by sov'ran gift possess. v. 366.
Had rounded still th' Horizon, and not known. x. 684.
To a fell Adversar*ie, hi*s hate or shame. x. 906.
And left t*o he*r self, if evil thence ensue. ix. 1185.

§ Poetic Elision of the semivowels.

It has been shown that the poetic elision (synalœpha) of naked vowels between words, is only a natural extension of the similar treatment in common speech of the same vowels within the word: and so it can be shown that the elision of the semivowels has an exact counterpart in our habitual treatment of certain other monosyllables, which I have called hypermonosyllables.

Semi-vocalic hyper-mono-syllables.

The words *schism*, *prism*, *chasm*, *spasm*, are usually reckoned to be monosyllables, and thus the finals of *baptism*, *abysm*, *despotism*, *paroxysm*, *&c. &c.*; a few examples will illustrate this. It should be noted that in all these words the vowel is short. Thus *schism* is a much shorter word than *size-'m* would make.

Of Baptisms, Sunday-schools and graves.
Shelley, *Peter Bell*, vi. 615.
Murmur'd this pious baptism—Be thou called. *Œd.* i. 360.

*In the dark backward and abysm of time. *Tempest*, i. 2. 50.
*Into the abysm of Hell. If he mistake. *A. & C.* iii. 13. 147.
Or sun from many a prism within the cave.
Shelley, *R. of I.* vii. 20.
As from a thousand prisms and mirrors, fills. *Epip.* 166.
*Of Newton with his prism and silent face. Wordsworth.
And filled with frozen light the chasms below.
Shelley, *Ath.* 269.
To other lands, leave azure chasms of calm.
Shelley, *Epip.* 466.
And where its chasms that flood of glory drank.
Laon. xi. (4245).
O'er chasms with new-fallen obstacles bestrown.
Words., *Eccl. Son.* ii. 12.

their typical phonetic condition

Now taking *prism* for type, and analysing it, we find that we do not combine the *sm* as in *small*, but vocalize the *m* separately. It may be represented to the eye as *pris'm* : there is some vocalic sound between the *s* and the *m* ; and it is thus just like *heaven* and *prison*, which are *hev'n* and *pris'n* : and *heaven* is freely used in all verse both as disyllable and monosyllable. *Seven* is a monosyllable in Chaucer and Milton, and Milton uses *prison* in the same way ; and we may ask what difference there is between these words and *battle*, or *temple*, which are *bat'l* and *temp'l*. If any distinction should be drawn between *pris'm* and *pris'n*, then *pris'm* is the longer. As for *l*, if that have any greater claim to be recognized as syllabic above *m* or *n* in *prism* and *prison*, this perhaps is because *l* is the most difficult sound for children to learn, and its quality may therefore have some natural tendency to be delayed. Milton's practice is this, that the unaccented vowels of syllables closed by *r*, *l*, or *n*, are elidible before another vowel, as freely as if they were 'naked'. *m* is not admitted so freely, if at all.

* In the starred examples there is correct Miltonic elision (as he has *spasm* in xi. 481), not in the others. Shelley uses *chasm* very frequently, and prefers it before a vowel, or at end of line, but has many purely monosyllabic examples.

In the semivowel elisions which will now be illustrated, the syllabic loss within the word is of course much more real (i.e. the shortening is more possible), if the consonant that precedes the *l*, *n*, or *r*, can be amalgamated with it, so as to be pronounced together with it and without break, as *wand'ring* is very easy, because the *dr* can be spoken together. But this facility is not required for poetic elision. *Glimmering* and *murmuring* are elidible although *mr* is a very awkward combination. *Glimmering* is easier than *glimring*, and therefore is no longer, while the second *u* in *murmuring* is so essential to the word, that if it were really cut out by 'elision' it would be bad writing to 'elide' it. Again, *lr* is almost impossible, and *artill'ry* (ii. 715) is in itself a sufficient refutation of the notion that all poetic elisions are common speech contractions; if it had been so, then some of Milton's elisions would never have been tolerated by him.

Syllabic value of semi-vowels.

As the inconsistent or uncertain values of the *power* and *fire* words were illustrated by examples from other poets, so the tendency to give syllabic value to semi-vowels in words where common speech usually treats them as asyllabic, may be seen in the following quotations:

> O how this spring of love resemb-l-eth. Shakespeare.
> And death's dark chasm̈, hurrying to and fro.
> Shelley, *Hellas*, 203.
> Filling the abyss with sunlike light-n-ings. *Prom.* iv. 276.
> Like hues and harmonies of eve-n-ing. *Int. Beauty.*
> Round which Death laughed, sepulchred emb-l-ms. *Pr.* 294.
> The dazz-l-ing sunrise; two sisters sweet. Keats.
> Turn'd syllab-l-ing thus: Ah Lycius bright.
> The parts and graces of the wrest(e)ler.
> Sh., *As Y. L.* ii. 2. 13.
> While she did call me rascal fidd(e)ler. *T. of S.* ii. 1. 158.
> You, the great toe of this assemb(e)ly. *Cor.* i. 1. 159.
> That croaks the fatal ent-e-rance of Duncan. *Mac.* i. 5. 40.
> A rotten case abides no hand(e)ling. 2 *H. IV.* iv. i. 161.

And strength by limping sway disab(e)led. *Sonn.* 66.
But who is man that is not ang(e)ry. *T. of A.* iii. 5. 56.[1]

Rule of R.

Syllabic loss with R.

If two unstressed vowels be separated by *r* there may be 'elision'; that is, the two syllables may count for one, the syllabic loss falling on the first of the two. These *r*-words are very numerous and suffer syllabic contraction in common speech: but though the spelling is often misleading to the eye, Milton did not always wish to mitigate it: it is as if he insisted on the syllable when he prints:

Lab*ou*ring had rais'd, and thus to Eve replied. x. 1012.

Examples are the following:

Nectarous, weltering, suffering, glimmering, murmuring, labouring, neighbouring, honouring, endeavouring, measuring, disfiguring, &c., mineral, general, several, artillery, desperate, deliberate, emperour, amorous, timorous, torturer, savoury, conqueror, &c.

Not distant far from thence a murmuring sound. iv. 453.
Luxuriant; mean while murmuring waters fall. 260.
Murmuring, and with him fled the shades of night. 1015.

These are quoted in Milton's spelling, and it is some evidence that he did not even degrade the affected vowel in pronunciation: and thus are

A Pill*ar o*f State; deep on his Front engraven. ii. 302.
Before them in a Cloud, and Pill*ar o*f Fire.
By day a Cloud, by night a Pill*ar o*f Fire. xii. 202. 3.

1 These last examples are from Abbott's *Shakespearian Grammar*. I would refer the reader to his sections on the lengthening and shortening of words which he finds necessary in order to make some of Shakespeare's lines scan. Quite apart from the disastrous uncertainty of rhythm which many of his examples exhibit, I find that I often prefer the very most ragged irregularity (which his explanations are designed to avoid) to the effect of torturing a word to make the verse scan. In the face of this experience, no one can deny the advantage of a fixed prosody, such as the French have observed. Lawlessness means uncertainty of rhythm, and that is the ruin of the verse.

All Judgement, wheth*er in* Heav'n, or Earth, or Hell. x. 57.
Celestial, wheth*er a*mong the Thrones, or nam'd. xi. 296.
Carnation, Purple, Az*ure, o*r spect with Gold. ix. 429.
With spots of Gold and Purple, az*ure, a*nd green. vii. 479.
The sav*our o*f Death from all things there that live. x. 269.

Note the pure *r* occurring in adjectives in *able* as *tolerable*, *miserable*, does not take elision, because with Milton the *a* was a long vowel with a secondary stress. It therefore naturally took a stress place in the verse, see under elision of *l*: and the word *misery* is always three full syllables, which is its more expressive form.

The rule of L.

with L.

When unstressed vowels are separated by *l*, they may suffer 'elision' like the *r*-words above, examples are: *popular*, *populous*, *articulate*, *credulous*, *groveling*, *perilous*—which last should not be considered as losing its *i* in a burr of the *r* as *parlous*—

Ex. As one who long in pop*ulo*us City pent. ix. 445.

This elision is freely used in the terminations of words, especially of adjectives in *able*, the penultimate being a long vowel with a secondary accent, and the *ble* being treated as pronounced, that is as a vocalized liquid, *áb'l*.

Examples:

His Temple right against the Temp*le o*f God. i. 402.
Wandring, shall in a glorious Temp*le e*nshrine. xii. 334.
Arraying with reflected Purp*le a*nd Gold. iv. 596.
Impenitrab*le*, impal'd with circling fire. ii. 647.
The Portal shon, inimitab*le o*n Earth. iii. 508.
Inextricab*le, o*r strict necessity. v. 528.
Son in whose face invisib*le i*s beheld. vi. 681.
To none communicab*le i*n Earth or Heaven. vii. 124.
Invisibl*e e*lse above all Starrs, the Wheele. viii. 135.
Foe not informidab*le, e*xempt from wound. ix. 486.
Inhospitab*le a*ppeer and desolate. xi. 306.
Distinguishab*le i*n member, joynt, or limb. ii. 668.

Elision of '-able'.

Adjectives in *-ble* which seem to offer an alternative elision in the middle of the word, as *miserable*, suffer the elision of the termination preferably to the other. This should be noticed, because since the penultimate has become shortened the practice has changed, so that a reader to-day will often mistake the prosody which frequently involves the rhythm.

Examples are :

Innumerab*le*. As when the potent Rod. i. 338. viii. 297.
Of depth immeasurab*le* : *A*non they move. i. 549.
More tollerab*le* ; *i*f there be cure or charm. ii. 460.
To be invulnerab*le* in those bright Arms. ii. 812.
Hung amiab*le*, *He*sperian Fables true. iv. 250.
So unimaginab*le* *a*s hate in Heav'n. vii. 54.
They view'd the vast immeasurab*le* *A*byss. vii. 211.
Abominab*le*, *a*ccurst, the house of woe. x. 465.
O miserab*le* *o*f happie ! is this the end. x. 720. 981.
His heart I know, how variab*le* *a*nd vain. xi. 92.
Deeds to thy knowledge answerab*le*, *a*dd Faith. xii. 582.
Abominab*le* *i*nutterab*le* *a*nd worse. ii. 626.

The proof that this was Milton's intention is merely the fact that such words only occur either firstly with their full syllabic value, and this very frequently, as :

Thy praises, with th' innumerable sound. iii. 147.
Me miserable ! which way shall I flie. iv. 73. x. 930.
Insuperable highth of loftiest shade. iv. 138.
Rafael, the sociable Spirit that deign'd. v. 221.
Innumerable as the Starrs of Night. v. 742. vi. 508.
Things not reveal'd, which th' invisible King.
vii. 122. (see p. 58)
Of men innumerable, there to dwell. vii. 156. 400.
To make her amiable : On she came. viii. 484.
Ye Cedars, with innumerable boughs. ix. 1089.
Inseparable must with mee along. x. 250.
Not unagreeable to found a path. x. 256.
Unutterable, which the spirit of prayer. xi. 6.
O miserable Mankind, to what fall. xi. 497.

And thus is to be scanned and read

Th*e* *u*ntractable Abysse, plung'd in the womb. x. 476

and

To human sense | th' invi|sible exploits. v. 565.

where the elision is determined by the text, and the following where it is not

> Then misera|ble *to have* | eternal being. ii. 98.
> Shoots invisi|ble ver|*tue even* to | the deep. iii. 586.

for which line see p. 35.

> Of somthing not unseasona|ble t*o a*sk. viii. 201.

or secondly before a vowel, as in examples on p. 31, or thirdly at the end of the line where they give an extrametrical syllable or hanger, e.g.

> Fall'n Cherube! to be weak is miserable. i. 157.
> Bristl'd with upright beams innumerable. vi. 82.
> Where boldest; though to sight unconquerable. vi. 118.
> Of all our good, sham'd, naked, miserable. ix. 1139 &c.

which are all like this unelidible

> Obscur'd, where highest Woods impenetrable. ix. 1086.

One exception.

I have only found one exception, namely the following line:

> Innumerable before th' Almighties Throne. iv. 585.

which I should consider an error of the text.

[§ Note on the word *Evil.*

('evil')

In Shakespeare the word *evil* is sometimes contracted, and it has been asserted that this contraction was due to loss of the *v* and a pronunciation *eel.* But with regard to Milton's use, the facts are that *Evil* occurs some forty times uncontracted, and about eight times besides at the end of lines (uncontracted), while of the eight times that it suffers contraction or elision seven are before a vowel, and thus bring the word under the rule of final *l.*[1] Besides this, Milton has written *knowledge of good and ill*, instead of *good and evil*, where the required elision is forbidden by a

[1] And Milton did not use the *v* contraction of *Even*, *e'en*, for he prints *Ev'n*, as he does *Heav'n*; and thus *Eev'ning* and *Eev'n*, and *Seav'n* for *seven*, see under N.

consonant. It will, therefore, be more regular to consider the following line,

> Both good and evil; good lost and evil got. ix. 1072.

as an error of the scribe or the printer for *evil and good*, which gives a better verse.]

The rule of N in elision.

Unstressed vowels separated by *n* suffer syllabic loss, as in these words: *business*, *hardening*, *original*, *opening*, *countenance*, *luminous*, *ominous*, *threatening*, *brightening*, *deafening*, *libidinous*, *unreasoning*.

Syllabic loss with N.

and thus between words:

> Whom reas*on h*ath equald, force hath made supream. i. 248.
> For those rebellious, here their Pris*on o*rdained. i. 71.
> Of massie Ir*on or* solid Rock with ease. ii. 878.
> Earth and the Gard'n of God, with Cedars crownd. v. 260.
> Our own begott*en*, *a*nd of our Loines to bring. x. 983.

Final N sometimes asyllabic.

But Milton frequently treats the final syllabic semivowel *n* as asyllabic, according to the analogy of *Heav'n*, *schism*, as explained above. Thus past participles in *en* are often contracted before consonants, e.g. *fall'n*, *ris'n*, *driv'n*, *chos'n*, *giv'n*, *eat'n*, *forbidd'n* (ix. 904), and the words *iron* and *prison* are each of them used once as monosyllables before a consonant:

> Out of such prison, though Spirits of purest light. vi. 660.
> With radiant light, as glowing Iron with fire. iii. 594.

The pronunciation *iern* would be like *fires* in ii. 709, &c.

The termination *-ion* seems to have been respected for its glide as unelidible (?).

Seven and *even* follow the use of *Heav'n*.

The last treatment of final *n* cannot be classed under Elision. The account of it is given above pp. 26–7. The simplest example is *heav'n*, and Milton, in following the native tradition of the contraction of such words, seems to have logically extended it.

§ Exceptions to the above rules of Elision.

('capital.') The exceptions to the above rules are few. The word *capital* loses its short *i* in ii. 924, xi. 343 and xii. 383, as its related *Capitoline* in ix. 508; and the following line is strictly out of rule,

> With thir bright Luminaries that Set and Rose. vii. 385.

unless we suppose that Milton omitted the secondary accent in the word *luminaries*. The word occurs in only two other places in *P. L.*, and there at the end of the line where it will take either accent equally well.

The scansion of the word *spirit* is exceptional.

(' spirit.') Milton uses the word *spirit* (and thus its derivatives) to fill indifferently one or two places of the ten in his verse (e.g. i. 17 and 101). The first vowel cannot suffer elision under the rule of pure *r*, because it is stressed. The word is an exception. It commonly discards one *i*, the question is which. It might be the first, for the old French *espirit*, whence our word immediately derives, has become *esprit*, and we have a form *sprite*. But Milton would have written this; and we may be confident that he suppresses the second vowel, following the Italian, e.g.

> Mentre che l' uno spir'to questo disse. *Inf.* v. 139.

These exceptions point to the weakness of the unaccented short *i*, which claims attention in the verse of *Sam. Ag.* see p. 47.

§ Arbitrary use of optional 'elision'.

Elision optional. There are two points to observe in Milton's manner of using his rules of elision. First, that the rules being in every case only permissive, he indicates no rule for their use; their application is arbitrary. We read on the same page:

> T'whom Mi|chael thus, | hee al-|so moved, | repli'd. xi. 453.
> To whom | thus Mi|cha-el; | Death thou | hast seen. 466.

Again, after

The im|age of | a brute, i. 371.

we have

Th' image | of God | in man, | crea|ted once.
xi. 508 and cp. vii. 527.

Again, the substantive *Being* suffers elision,

That gave | thee being, | stil shades | thee, and | protects.
ix. 266.

while the less important participle has sometimes its full value,

His violence | thou fearst | not, be|-ing such | ix. 282, etc., etc.

Secondly, that Milton came to scan his verses in one way, and to read them in another.

§ Scansion divorced from the rhythm.

Rhythm not prosodial.

Thus I wrote, as appears in previous editions; but what I intended is ill-expressed, and has not been understood. I will, therefore, explain at length.

The intended rhythm in *P. L.* is always given by the unmitigated accentuation of the words of the verse as Milton pronounced them; nor does the qualification 'as he pronounced them' raise much uncertainty. One use of a prosody, and his is no exception, is to ensure the right values of the words which give the rhythms. Thus in the line

Shóots invísible vírtue éven to the déep.

there are five accents, the places of which are absolutely determined by the speech accents; but the verse when thus read is very bold, and to many readers does not seem like a blank verse at all: and Milton could not have written it except by virtue of his prosody, which allows him to invert the accent of any foot and make free use of his fiction of elision. He here allows himself to invert the first, second, and fourth feet, and if we substitute a monosyllable for the word *virtue*, which theoretically dissolves its second syllable in the synalœpha, we get,

Shoots in|visi|ble rays | ev'n to | the deep,

which is a perfectly regular line if we accept the inversions as Milton intended us to do. But when we come to scan the original line we find that we have to accept | *tue even to* | as a foot unit in the disyllabic metre, and that is a pretty stiff fiction :

Shoots in|visi|ble vir|tue even to | the deep.

Again we must read the line,

Of Ráinbows and Stárrie Eýes the Wáters thús,

as here accented, but if we scan it, we find that one of the feet in the scansion is | starry eyes | and it carries two of the five accents undoubtedly present :

Of rain|bows and | starry ' eyes | the wa|ters thus.

Again these two lines beginning,

The image | of God
The sa|vour of death|.

are identical in rhythm, but different in their prosodial explanation. Perhaps this condition of things is expressed by saying that the rhythm overrides the prosody that creates it. The prosody is only the means for the great rhythmical effects, and is not exposed but rather disguised in the reading.

[§] Of Contractions.

Contracted participles, &c.

Milton uses the ordinary speech contraction of the preterites and participles in *ed* which he often writes *t*, and the following should be noted,

Confus'dly, and which thus must ever fight. ii. 914.

for, without his spelling, the optional terminal elision would have been read with satisfaction.

He seems also to have preferred the contracted form of the termination of the second person singular of verbs, writing not only *thinkst*, *seekst*, *spakst*, *sawst*, *dwellst*, *&c.*, but even *eatst*, *foundst*, *commandst*, and prefers *rememberst* to *remembrest*, *openst* to *op'nest*, as his theory compelled *revisitst* for *revis'test*; all which last seem to me detestable and indefensible.

The similar superlative termination of adjectives was not unfrequently contracted by Shakespeare. Milton does not contract this, and in the following line,

> Created hugest that swim th' Ocean stream. i. 202.

forbids it by an apostroph elsewhere, but there is one exception in *P. R.*

> Severest temper, smooth the rugged'st brow. ii. 164.

He uses the common poetical contractions *o'er* for *over*, *e'er* for *ever*, in *whatever* and *wherever*, but he does not favour the ordinary contraction of *in the*, *of the*, *&c.*, which is frequent in Shakespeare as his verse becomes more accentual. The exception *i' th' midst* i 224 and

(ith' midst).

> Ith' midst an Altar as the Land-mark stood. xi. 432.

stand alone: see note D.]

II. *Variety in number of stresses.*

Rationale of blank verse.

The following questions as to the number and position of stresses in syllabic blank verse belong honestly to rhythm rather than to prosody: and if there were any accepted theory of the rhythm of blank verse, it should be possible to class every case under some one rhythmical type; but this is impossible in the absence of any commanding theory. And if it were possible it might prove too cumbersome and elaborate for practical use; while in so far as it were practical its rules might be reckoned prosodial, like the rules for word-units in the classical caesuras, &c.

It is certain that blank verse is agreeable on account of its rhythm, and it is also certain that its rhythms vary. It would therefore follow that it has several types of rhythm, and the first step in analysis should be to distinguish these one from another, when it would probably appear that they were distinguished by the positions of their main accents, which might be three essential places and one subsidiary or movable, the fifth accent being negligible. Each type would have subvarieties due to 'inversions' of its essential accents and to differences in the unessential places. In such an explanation, which was suggested to me by Mr. Rafael Piccoli before he left us for the War, the line of five equal accents—which is assumed in this treatise as the normal—would stand apart from the main types, and be normal only in the sense that it combined the types by containing the essential regular accents of each one of them. In such a laborious investigation, the tabulation of Milton's and Dante's rhythms should offer the best groundwork.

Lines of five accents.

1. Examples of lines with five full accents were given on p. 1: and it may be noted that accentual blank verse differs from syllabic blank verse in this, that it always has five accents in the line.

In the following examples, the unaccented or weak 'feet' are distinguished by italic type.

of four accents.

2. Lines with only four accents:

The omitted accent may be the first e.g.

> *As from* the Center thrice to th' utmost Pole. i. 74.
> *And in* luxurious Cities where the noyse. i. 498.

The effect of this is always to weaken the line. It is, therefore, rare, and it is only in long poems that it can be used with good effect.

Initial weak feet are, like the examples above, almost always made up of two monosyllables, and a slight accent will be given in reading to the first of them, so that the foot is really inverted; see p. 41 on inversions, and on inversions of the first foot. Thus I think we should most of us read the last quotation with a slight stress on the conjunction and none on the preposition. As to whether the prepositions had more stress value in Milton's time, so as to forbid this rhythm, see p. 79. The conjunction *and* often occurs in stress-places in Milton's verse, where stressing it would make the verse ridiculous. See *P. R.* I. lines 99-109.

The stress may fail in the second place,

> Serv'd on*ly to* discóver síghts of wóe. i. 64.
> Nor sérv'd *it to* relàx their sérried filés. vi. 599.

In the third place,

> A Dúngeon hórr*ible*, on áll sides róund. i. 61.

In the fourth place,

> Sole reígning hólds the Týr*anny* of Héav'n. i. 124.

In the fifth place,

> No líght, but ráther dárkness vis*ible*. i. 63.

The last accent.

On p. 84 Tyrwhitt is quoted as saying that one of the indispensable conditions of English blank verse was that the last syllable should be strongly accented. The truth seems to be that its metrical position in a manner exonerates it from requiring any accent.—Whether the 'last foot' may be inverted is another question.—A weak syllable can very well hold its own in this tenth place, and the last essential accent of the verse may be that of the 'fourth foot'. The analogy with the dipody of the classical iambic, and with the four-minim bar of the old *alla breve* time in music is evident.

Lines with three accents.

3. Some lines have only three full stresses,

> His Mín*isters* of véng*eance and* pursúit. i. 170.
> The Sój*ourners* of Gósh*en*, *who* behéld. i. 309.
> Transfíx *us to* the bott*om of* this Gúlfe. i. 329.

The conclusion is that there is no one place in the verse where an accent is indispensable.

Never more than five.

There cannot be more than five metrical accents in one line. If the regular five accents are all present no heaviness of the syllables in the unaccented places can make another, though it may make bad verses. The line often quoted to disprove this rhythmical truth,

> Rocks, Cáves, Lakes, Féns, Bogs, Déns and Shádes of Deáth,
> ii. 621.

is to be read as here accented; and if the heavy syllables between these accents are themselves stressed, then the accented syllables will, by the enforcing of voice-tone, be able to subordinate them. The intention was, of course, to make a line as heavy and obstructive as possible; the rhythmical accents being aided by rhyme and alliteration.

III. *Of inversion of feet.*

Inversion of accent in any place.

Blank verse is typically in rising rhythm; i.e. the metric accent is regularly on the even syllables, but the rhythm is sometimes falling; i.e. the accent may be shifted on to the odd syllable in any place in the line; it is then described as inverted.

Inversions of accent in all places except the first disturb the rhythm so as to call attention to the word which carries the irregular accent or stress: they are, therefore, used primarily in relation to the sense (see the following examples (a)). But in a long poem like *P. L.* the more common inversions soon become as familiar to the ear as is the typical rhythm; they then fall into the condition of the inversion of the first foot, and enliven the rhythm without taxing the sense (see the following examples (b)).

Inversion is most common in the first foot, next in the third and fourth, very rare in second, and most rare in fifth.

§ Inversions of first foot.

This inversion does not affect the sense, but it freshens the rhythm, e.g.

> Régions of sorrow, doleful shades, where peace. i. 65.

As a general rule, when the first foot is weak, it will strengthen itself by a slight conventional inversion in spite of the sense, e.g.

> We shall be free. i. 259.

This behaviour of the initial foot will also account for any inversion which follows a period in the sense.

§ Inversion of second foot.

> (*a*) A mind nót to be chang'd by Place or Time. i. 253.
> (*a*) Mee mee ónely just object of his ire. x. 936.
> To the Gárden of Bliss, thy seat prepar'd. viii. 299.
> In the Vísions of God: It was a Hill. xi. 377.

§ Inversion of third foot.

> (*a*) For one restraint, Lórds of the World besides? i. 32.
> (*b*) Which tasted works knówledge of Good and Evil. vii. 543.

§ Inversion of fourth foot.

> (*a*) Illumine, what is low raise and support. i. 23.
> (*a*) As when two Polar Winds blówing adverse. x. 289.
> Before thy fellows, ambítious to win. vi. 160.
> (*b*) From Noon, and gentle Aires dúe at thir hour. x. 93.

§ Inversion of fifth foot.

Rarity of fifth inversion.

This is very rare, and does not so much emphasize the word which carries it, as it imparts strangeness to the sentence, well used in the following examples:

> Beyond all past example and fúture. x. 840.
> Which of us who beholds the bright súrface. vi. 472.

Some poets say that this rhythm is impossible, and was not intended; and would accent future and surfàce on the last; and so they must accent *prostràte* in

> Of Thrones and mighty Seraphim próstrate. vi. 841.

though Milton always uses *fúture* and *próstrate*, and there is said to be no other example of *surfáce* in literature. If it be argued that these words, being compounds or Latin, do not forbid the distortion, it may be that they were chosen to give such readers an option; and this would cover

> Spoild Principalities and Powers, triumpht. x. 186.

as this word can be accented either way. See *Comus*, 974.

But the first of the examples quoted above is a very beautiful effect and the second is descriptive. Keats used this inversion deliberately and markedly in an important and typical place,

> Bright star, would I were steadfast as thou art,

and it would have been strange if Milton had never used its rhythm, for there are several ways by which it is naturally arrived at; first from Chaucer's use of French words in this place, and secondly our reading of classical iambic verse, in which it is very familiár: and I am convinced that the frequency of inversion in the first foot is historically due to the common presence of a disyllable at the beginning of the Latin iambic which came to be universally familiar in the Latin church hymns.

The above inversions, as all other variations of rhythm, owe their value to the presupposed metrical type from which they vary; but they must not be disguised by reading a conventional stress in the regular place. They determine the rhythm, nor is the metre falsified by them, because the interruption is not long enough, and the majority of verses sustain the impression of the typical form.

§ Multiple inversions.

There may be more than one inversion in the same line.

Falling feet freely used.

Examples of inversion of first and second feet: which was enforced in *Sam. Ag.* See p. 56.

> (*a*) U'nivérsal reproach, far worse to beare. vi. 34.
> Bý the wâters of Life, where ere they sate. xi. 79.

of third and fourth,

> (*a*) As a despite doń agaińst the most High. vi. 906.

of the second and fourth,

> In thir tríple Degrees, Régions to which. v. 747.

In these last two examples the weak first foot is also inverted.

¶ *Remarks on the break in the verse.*

Cæsura.

Like the classic metres which have the caesura fixed by rule, a blank verse in English tends to divide itself into two balancing parts; and a natural rhythmical division may generally be felt in lines which contain no grammatical pause. But where there is any grammatical pause it is that which determines the break.

Now since blank verse is a system of short sentences of all possible variety of length, fitted within the frame of a five-foot metre, the tendency of the break towards the middle part of the verse is easily lost; and when the verse is handled in a masterly manner the break may occur well in any part of the line. It is necessary, therefore, to discard the word caesura, with its precise signification, and call this division in blank verse 'the break'.

In the following illustrations consider the verse as of ten syllabic units, and the break to occur between the two components of ten which are given to represent the verse; thus,

1 2 3 4 5 6 7 8 9 10
Of man's first dis-o-be-dience, and the fruit [7+3]

is a 7+3 line: i.e. the break occurs between the seventh and eighth syllables: seven before it and three after.

Here is an example of the relation between sentences and metre in an elaborate passage. The following sentences:

... Harmonious numbers;	5 syllables.
As the wakeful Bird sings darkling,	8 "
And in shadiest Covert hid	7 "
Tunes her nocturnal Note.	6 "
Thus with the Year Seasons return,	8 "
But not to me returns Day,	7 "
Or the sweet approach of Ev'n or Morn,	9 "

make the verses

Harmonious numbers; as the wakeful Bird [5+5]
Sings darkling, and in shadiest Covert hid [3+7]
Tunes her nocturnal Note. Thus with the Year [6+4]
Seasons return, but not to me returns [4+6]
Day, or the sweet approach of Ev'n or Morn. iii. 42. [1+9]

the above and the following give examples of all the nine single breaks,

Joyn voices all ye living Souls, ye Birds. v. 197. [8+2]
... Firm they might have stood,
Yet fell; remember, and fear to transgress. vi. end. [2+8]
... Such as in thir Soules infix'd
Plagues; they astonisht all resistance lost. vi. 838. [1+9]
And Bush with frizl'd hair implicit: last [9+1]
Rose as in Dance the stately Trees. vii. 323.

In the last three examples the break emphasizes the sense. The early defenders of *P. L.* when still fewer than fit, were scandalized by the verse 1+9.

§ Double breaks.

There are sometimes two breaks in a line: the variety and severity of the breaks is a distinction of Milton's verse. The following are some examples. It is not always possible to say whether a verse has one or two breaks; readers would differ.

Broken verses.

> Hail Son of God, Saviour of Men, thy Name. iii. 412. [4+4+2]
>
> Instruct me, for Thou know'st; Thou from the first. i. 19. [3+3+4]
>
> Shall grieve him, if I fail not, and disturb. i. 167. [3+4+3]
>
> Of God, as with a Mantle didst invest. iii. 10. [2+5+3]
>
> Regions of sorrow, doleful shades, where peace. [5+3+2]

These are indications of the varieties, which are numberless; for when the metrical components of a verse are parts of sentences, the other parts of which go to the composition of the next verses before and after, the breaks of such verses cannot be considered apart: and were these varieties exhausted, the variations of these, as effected by the position of weak or inverted stresses, would remain to reckon, before the changes possible in the mere formal rhythm, apart from all that is introduced by the language, were enumerated. It is few who will pursue this path any further.

P.S.—It should be added that any consideration of Milton's rhythm or versification in *P. L.* should exclude those passages where he follows the Authorized Version of the Bible—especially where the speaker is the Deity. Reverence for the text has made him insert it almost unaltered, the lines are often bad, and one of them does not scan at all. The justification does not lie in the prosody. The occasional intrusion of a foreign force refractory to the main current has the effect of powerfully enhancing the value of the normal conditions. Dante got this effect by the use of Latin quotations in his carefully versified poem; and perhaps Milton might have done better if he could have used the Vulgate instead of the vernacular version.

PART II

ON THE PROSODY OF

PARADISE REGAINED

AND

SAMSON AGONISTES

Paradise Regained and *Samson Agonistes* were written some time after the completion of *Paradise Lost*, and the examination of their metre and rhythm is therefore of great interest, as it must divulge to us whether Milton was satisfied with the rules by which he had bound himself in his long poem ; and, if he was not, in what direction he was inclined to alter them. Such an inquiry will show that Milton did not keep quite strictly to his laws of 'elision', but that he approved of the great rhythmical experiments which he had made, and extended these.

Method of enquiry.

In examining these two poems, I shall arrange the matter in two chapters ; in the first I will give all the examples which show departure from the rules of prosody tabulated from *P. L.* This must be somewhat tedious, but it is necessary, and fortunately not a very long affair ; in the second I will give an account of the metrical and rhythmical system of *Samson*, which contains Milton's most elaborate and artificial versification.

¶ *On the relaxation which is found in Paradise Regained and Samson Agonistes of the laws of 'Elision' so called in Paradise Lost.*

There are not all together a score of exceptions to the rules tabulated in Part I of this book. None of the following lines would have been admitted into *P. L.*

Exceptions to rules of *P. L.*

(1) Thy poli*ti*c maxims, or that cumbersome. *P. R.* iii. 400.
(2) The rest was magnanim*ity* to remit, *S.* 1470.
(3) And he in that calam*ito*us prison left. *S.* 1480.

(4) In slavish hab*it*, ill-fitted weeds. *S.* 122.

(5) With youthful courage and magnan*im*ous thoughts. *S.* 524.
(6) She's gone, a man*if*est Serpent by her sting. *S.* 997.
(7) But provi*de*nce or instínct of nature seems. *S.* 1545.

(8) And all the flour*ish*ing works of peace destroy. *P.R.* iii. 80.
(9) Wilt thou then serve the Phil*ist*ines with that gift. *S.* 577.

(10) Sok't in his en*em*ies blood, and from the stream. *S.* 1726.

(11) Present in temples at idol*atr*ous rites. *S.* 1378.
(12) Drunk with Idol*atr*y, drunk with Wine. *S.* 1670.

(13) Justl*y*, *y*et despair not of his final pardon. *S.* 1171.
(14) Whose off-spring in his Territor*y y*et serve. *P. R.* iii. 375.

(15) To something extr*ao*rdinary my thoughts. *S.* 1383.
(16) Out, out H*yæ*na; these are thy wonted arts. *S.* 748.

Of these examples the first three are of unaccented *ĭ* before *t*, and are like the exception of *capital* in *P. L.* This *ĭt* is the shortest of all the true syllables made by a vowel and a consonant. No. 4 is the same condition terminal before a vowel (p. 63 foot). Nos. 5, 6, 7 are *ĭ* before other consonants, while 8 and 9 are again *ĭ*, but under obstructed conditions which make contraction of the syllable quite abhorrent to the style of *P. L.*

No. 10 if taken with 5 would seem to point to admission of *m* into the rules of *l*, *n* and *r*; and this might be a reasonable extension.

Nos. 11 and 12 are best accounted for by supposing that the word *idolatry* had acquired a familiar contracted pronunciation in Puritan talk, and that it pleased Milton to adopt this.

Nos. 13 and 14 are easy enough synaloephas of a final vocalic *y* with initial consonantal *y*.

Nos. 15 and 16 require special discussion.

To these lines may be added

('misery.') (17) The close of all my *miseries*, and the balm. *S.* 651.

because in *P. L.* this word *misery* always fills three places in the verse: and the word-unit suffers in dignity by contraction, though that is prosodially admissible. And I must note the two following lines, which I admitted in my earlier book as exceptions, but would now explain differently: the first was

Two difficult lines.

(18) The worst of all indignities, yet on me. *S.* 1341.

I had reckoned this among the *ĭt* examples. The best scansion seems to be by recognition of the enclitic accent on *on* as in these lines

> That fault I take not ón me, but transfer. *S.* 241.
> Or rather flight, no great advantage ón me. *S.* 1118.

dividing the feet thus

> The worst | of all | indig|nities | yet on (me).

Again, nothing forbids the accent being on *yet*, except that the condition of an inverted fifth foot with an extra metrical syllable has no parallel in Milton.

The second was

(19) Some way or other yet further to afflict thee. *S.* 1252.

which I had by mere stupidity, as it seems to me now, classed with Nos. 13 and 14. It can be divided thus

(19) Some way | or o|ther yet | further | to ' afflict (thee).

inverting the fourth foot agreeably to the emphasis, though one would have expected the elision to be marked. Or we can suppose the Chaucerian speech-contraction of *other*, which has not come down to us, and this would be met half-way by the other examples of 'elision' with *yet* (Nos. 13 and 14).

Apologizing for these mistakes I will now reduce my older disquisitions on Nos. 15 and 16.

The first of these two lines should be scanned thus

('extra-ordinary.')

(15) To some|thing ex|tr*ao*rdi|nary | my thoughts.

that is with inversion of the third foot with a somewhat similar but weaker condition of the fourth, see example on p. 43. I shall show later, when dealing with the rhythms of *Samson*, that there is good reason for irregularity in this place (see note E). The 'elision' assumed in the pronunciation of *extraordinary* requires defence, because a philological journal of some repute (not English) has informed me that Milton said *extraornary*. If he had, he would have written it, but the Dutch scholar was ignorant that the word *extraordinary* did not follow the rule or habit of *ordinary*. This was commonly pronounced *ord'nary* and sometimes *ornary*, and the last form went to America: but *extraordinary* seems to have been a comparatively rare word, and I have seen no evidence of its similar contraction. Ellis gives *ornary* from Jones 1701, but *extraordinary* in full from Price, 1668. And in a book printed in 1694 '*Plautus's Comedies* . . . made English . . . printed for Abel Swalle', &c. there is a preface, in which the author says that he has used 'so many Abbreviations, to make it (the style) appear still more like common Discourse, and the usual way of speaking;' and he fears that 'the English must necessarily appear mean'. He is a scholar carefully representing usual low forms of speech by spellings 'that are not usual', and in his plays *ord'nary* occurs several times; but the word *extraordinary*, which he happens to use both in his preface and remarks, and also in his text, is spelt in full when he is himself speaking, while in the dialogue it is printed *extreordinary*.

> *Per.* This is extreordinary indeed. p. 94.

Indeed the objection to supposing this line to scan by 'elision' of the short *i* is that it suppresses the slight secondary accent of the full word, and suggests the conversational tone of speech inappropriate and forbidden to the situation (see p. 101, and note F).

('Hyæna.') In the second of these two exceptional lines we have apparently an extrametrical syllable, thus

Out out | Hyæ|(na) these are | thy won|ted arts

but as there is no other example of an extrametrical syllable within the line in all *P. L.*, *R.*, and *Samson*, we feel driven to make a prosodial synalœpha of the *yæ* of Hyæna, thus with inversion of second and third feet

Out out | H*yæ*na | these are | thy won|ted arts

Hyæna is an exceptional word, and it is italicized like the proper names in *Samson Agonistes*. Neither Chaucer nor Shakespeare recognize the final *a*. Chaucer has *hyene* with the very weak terminal *e* rhyming, *between*(*e*), *susten*(*e*), &c. Shakespeare has *hien*. If Milton used the Latin pronunciation of it, the synalœpha of the *ie* is natural enough.

The reader may draw his own conclusions from this summary of the exceptions found in *P. R.* and *Samson*, to the rules observed in *P. L.* It is plain that these later poems contain true exceptions to the rules observed in *P. L.* and if these be taken together with the liberties of Milton's earlier verse, and all his work be considered together, then its prosody will not appear to differ much from that of other writers: and it is that confusion which has obscured his definite intention and hidden his careful experiment from his commentators.

¶ *On the prosody and rhythm of Samson Agonistes.*

In *Samson*, there is lyric choral verse mixed in with the blank verse in the manner of a Greek drama, in which the elaborate choruses were very free and lyrical in rhythm.

Milton's main purpose in his later writing was to invent an English prosody which should be independant of rhyme, that is, using rhyme only as an ornament: and he shows in the choruses of *Samson* how the metric prosodial fictions of *P. L.* allow the disyllabic verse to take on a great variety of free rhythms—and this metric system has never been understood by his critics.[1]

Milton's intentions

It is a natural condition of rhythm, that the common rhythms should be familiar and popular, and they are probably fundamental, but after familiarity with them the ear soon grows dissatisfied and wishes them to be broken; it is only those who have no natural ear for rhythm, who can be charmed and contented with regularity, and they will resent any infraction of it; but those who love rhythm for its own sake know that it is not worth calling rhythm unless it is freely varied, and that rhythm truly begins to be beautiful only when the regularity is broken.

But this also is true, that some knowledge of the structure or laws that govern free rhythms in poetry are indispensable to most persons before they will receive them as melodious, and they will accept or reject a rhythm to which they are unaccustomed, according as they can or cannot perceive, or think they perceive, its structure [an actual example of this is given in note G]. Now this attitude towards beauty of any kind is not the best; but its cause in reading verse-rhythms is the true discomfort of uncertainty, and where there is any uncertainty there is a failure of rhythm. My undertaking is to get rid of this uncertainty, and to put the reader into such a comfortable and assured state of mind with regard

should be understood

[1] I believe that it is to Gerard Hopkins that the discovery is due.

to the structure of the verse in *Samson Agonistes*, as will enable him to encounter the rhythms with confidence. If, by explaining the prosody, I enable him to scan the verses, I expect that he will be able to enjoy the rhythms. If he still cannot do so, that may be my fault or his, it cannot be Milton's.

The present chapter will therefore be an account of the elemental structure of the verse of *Samson Agonistes*. I shall begin by getting rid of what I believe to be the chief source of misunderstanding.

Mixture of rising and falling feet common.

No one has ever found any difficulty in the metre or rhythm of the poems *L'Allegro* and *Il Penseroso.* In these poems, setting aside their irregular openings, there are two kinds of line, one the eight-syllable line with rising stress (so-called iambic), the other the seven-syllable line with falling stress (so-called trochaic), this latter being exactly like the former with the first syllable omitted. But if we examine a passage from one of these poems, we shall find that there is also a third kind of line, which intermediates between the other two types, and that this is made by the simple device of inverting the first foot of the eight-syllable line ; thus—

> And oft, | as if | her head | she bow'd,
> Stooping | through a | fleecy | cloud.
> Oft on | a Plat | of ri|sing ground,
> I hear | the far- | off *Cur*|*feu* sound,
> Over | som wide- | water'd | shoar,
> Swinging | slow with | sullen | roar.

Of these six lines, the first and fourth are regular eight-syllable lines with rising stress ('iambic'), and the second, fifth, and sixth are regular seven-syllable lines with falling stress ('trochaic') ; but the third is an eight-syllable line with the first stress inverted, or falling, and it begins as if it were going to be a seven-syllable line (trochaic) throughout, and it reads equally well (for the two things are identical) as a line of falling stress (trochaic) with a trisyllabic foot (so-called dactyl) in the first place. Its structure is

An ambiguity.

Oft′ on | a plát | of rí|sing gróund,

but by the inversion of the first foot it reads as if it were scanned thus

Oft′ on a | plát of | rísing | gróund.

Such an example as the above offers no difficulty, and it has never given rise to any difference of opinion as to its metrical device; but it is clear that if there was an optional elision in the first foot, it would not only be possible to take it in these two ways, but impossible to say which was the better explanation. If, for instance, we substitute such a disyllable as *Softly* for the words *Oft on*, thus

Softly a plat of rising ground,

it is clear that, according as we admit or refuse an elision of the open *y* before the *a*, we have a seven-syllable line with falling stress throughout, or an eight-syllable line of rising stress with the first foot inverted; that is either

Softl*y a* | plat of | rising | ground,

or

Softly | a plat | of ri|sing ground.

A verse in this condition is under no uncertainty of rhythm: there is no doubt how the verse is to be read and stressed, but there are two possible ways of explaining its metrical structure: and it is merely a matter of convenience in classification which one we take.

Now in *Samson* this condition occurs complicated by these further conditions, that the inversions are not confined to the first foot of the line, and the lines are of various lengths: and Milton has purposely used these liberties together, on account of their rhythmical resources, in order to introduce true trisyllabic rhythms into his verse, which is all the while composed strictly of disyllabic feet.

A mistake that I made in my previous edition will illustrate this complication. I quoted this line

(1) As a lingring disease. 618.

from a misprinted version in which *lingering* was given with the full trisyllabic value which Milton's spelling forbids. It therefore figured in my book among the falling lines.

Rising and falling systems

In such verse as I have quoted from *Il Penseroso*, where the eight-syllable and seven-syllable systems are mixed together, it is the method of some metrists to regard all the lines, whether rising or falling, as being composed of the same metrical units, and differing only by the insertion or not of an unaccented initial syllable. This way is very simple, and if rhythmic stress in poetry be regarded as equivalent to accent in musical rhythm, and the metrical units be counted as measured bars or half-bars, it may be used as an explanation. In Chaucer's ten-syllable verse, the first syllable is sometimes omitted—(just as it is in *L'Allegro* and *Il Penseroso*)—and those who prefer to look at the matter in this way, will thus explain the odd-syllable verse of *Samson*. But in proportion as the lines are invaded by inversions, the explanation ceases to be satisfactory, and I shall in this chapter always distinguish falling rhythms ('trochaic') from rising ('iambic') rhythms with inversions. The distinction is of more importance in analysis than the theoretic likeness, which stupidly neglects the striking difference of effect between rising and falling rhythms, which is perceived by all hearers, as the difference in the difficulty of writing them is known to all writers.

essentially distinct.

Now in *Samson Agonistes*, if all the lines of falling rhythm (so-called trochaic, or lines which lack the initial syllable) be recognized and separated from the rest,—and there are only seventeen in all the 1758,—it will be found that the whole of the poem, with those exceptions, is composed in rising rhythm, of regular disyllabic feet (so-called iambs) with free liberty of inversions, and of weak places, and of 'elisions', and of extrametrical syllables at the end of the line, all such as we found in *P. L.* The whole of the 'dactylic' and 'trochaic' effects are got by the placing of inversions, elisions, &c.; and where the 'iambic' system seems entirely to disappear, it is maintained as a fictitious structure and scansion, not intended to be read, but to be imagined as a time-beat on which the free rhythm is, so to speak, syncopated, as a melody.

True prosodic falling metre rare in *S. A.*

Firstly, these are the seventeen lines in falling rhythm: and they are all of them in the choric or lyric verse.

(2) Lét us | nót break | ín u|pón him. 116.
(3) Thát He|róick | thát Re|nówn'd. 125.
(4) Or the | sphéar of | fórtune | ráises. 172.
(5) O that | tórment | shoúld not | be con|fín'd. 606.
(6) To the | bódies | woúnds and | sóres. 607.
(7) Bút must | sécret | pássage | fínd. 610.
(8) As on | éntrails, | joínts, and | límbs. 614.
(9) And ce|léstial | vígour | árm'd. 1280.
(10) Gréat a|móng the | Héathen | róund. 1430.
(11) In the | cámp of | Dán. 1436.
(12) Whíle thir | héarts were | jócund | and sub|líme. 1669.
(13) Líke that | sélf-be|gótt'n | bird. 1699.
(14) Ín the A|rábian | wóods em|bóst. 1700.
(15) That no | sécond | knóws nor | thírd. 1701.
(16) All' is | bést, though | we oft | dóubt. 1745.
(17) Whát th' un|seárcha|ble dis|póse. 1746.
(18) Oft' he | séems to | híde his | fáce. 1749.

We may accept Mr. W. P. Ker's judgement that lines 713, 714, should be taken as one line, thus

(19) Comes this way sailing like a stately ship.

Of the above lines 5 and 12 are like Chaucer's nine-syllable lines; that is, if an initial syllable were added, they would be ordinary ten-syllable 'blank' verses. In 6 and 11, if contraction were allowed of the words *to the* and *in the*, these two lines could be reckoned as in rising rhythm; while 14 and 17, if the 'elisions' (marked in 17) be neglected, would become regular eight-syllable lines with an inversion of the first foot. But of these, number 11 is the only line in which the falling ('trochaic') rhythm can be doubted as the poet's intention (see note H).

Having dismissed these lines, the whole of the rest of the poem is to be explained as in rising disyllabic (iambic) metres, broken by inversions, &c.

Inversion of first two feet.

And first I will take all the instances of the most peculiar rhythm which is obtained by these inversions, that is when the first two feet of the line are inverted: here are the lines, eleven in number—

frequent examples.

(20) Írre|cóvera|bly dark, | tótal | Eclipse. 81.

In this verse there is also inversion of the fourth foot.

(21) Ór by e|vásions | thy críme | uncó|verst móre. 842.
(22) Írre|sisti|ble Sám|son? whóm | unárm'd. 126.
(23) Thát in|vínci|ble Sám|son, fár | renówn'd. 341.

(and compare with these two last

(24) Samson | should be | brought fórth | to shew | the péo(ple) 1601.)
(25) Úni|vérsal|ly crówn'd | with hígh|est prái(ses). 175.
(26) Fór his | péople | of óld; | what hín|ders nów? 1533.
(27) Ó how | cómely | it ís | and hów | reví(ving). 1268.
(28) Tó the | Spírits | of júst | men lóng | opprést. 1269.
(29) Púts in|vínci|ble míght | 1271.
(30) Ánd with | blíndness | intér|nal strúck | 1686.

and add to these examples 83 and 89 below.

I will say about each one of these lines what is to be urged against this view of their metrical construction: but first, in favour of the explanation that they are all instances of inversion of the first two feet, I will give examples of similar rhythm from *Paradise Lost* and *Regained*.

(31) Úni|vérsal | reproách, | far worse | to beare. *P. L.* vi. 34.
(32) Bý the | wáters | of Lífe, | where ere | they sate. xi. 79.
(33) Ín the | bósom | of blíss, | and light | of light. *R.* iv. 597.
(34) Tó the | Gárden | of bliss, | thy seat | prepar'd. *L.* viii. 299.
(35) Áfter | fórty | days fás|ting had | remain'd. *R.* ii. 243.
(36) Throúgh the | infi|nite Host, | nor less | for that. *L.* v. 871.
(37) Shóots in|vísi|ble vér|t*ue* éven to | the deep. *L.* iii. 586.

This has, like 20, an inversion also of the fourth foot. And add other examples given on p. 43 of inversions of the second foot with a weak first foot slightly inverted, and these less-marked lines

(38) Ádam, | well may | we la|bour still | to dress. ix. 205.
(39) Lábour, | as to | debarr | us when | we need. 236.
(40) Góing | into | such dan|ger as | thou saidst. 1157.

Of these ten lines from the epic verse, most of the examples are indubitable, and prove that the rhythm is one which we should expect to find; while the extreme pathos of it in ex. 20, where it is impossible to make any other rhythm, the fact that in 22, 23, 24 it is used as expressive of the bond-bursting Samson, the absolute necessity for allowing it in 30, and the appearance of it in those weaker examples connected with labour and danger, 38, 39 and 40, all together make a strong case for admitting the explanation to cover all the examples given, including that on p. 65.

an intentional effect.

But it may have been observed that in three of these 21 lines the words *irresistible* or *invincible* occur, and since 'elision' of the short *i* is allowed in *Samson* (see p. 47), it might be suspected here as a preferable explanation. And these examples, i. e. 22, 23, and 29, might, if there were no considerations to determine otherwise, be all scanned as odd-syllable lines containing elision of the short *i*; and thus

Ir|resis|t*i*ble Sam|son whom | unarmed.
That | invín|c*i*ble Sam|son far | renowned.

would be Chaucerian nine-syllable lines, just like

examples 5 and 12 above from the chorus. But this, as I said before, makes no difference to the rhythm: the chief objection to such an explanation is that it does not explain all the lines. It is true that examples 25, 26, 27, 28, 34, 36, and 37, are in the same condition with these other four, for these lines also all contain a possible elision or contraction: but the contraction of *univers'lly* in 25 would be unparalleled, and examples 20, 21, 30, 31, 32, 33 and 35, which are all decided cases, would still be left: so that it is more convenient to group them together as above.

prejudice against it.

But no metrical explanation which does not falsify the rhythm is in itself objectionable; what is wrong is to read these lines *Irrécoverábly, Irrésistìble, That ìn-vincīble* or *cĭbble, Unìversàlly, O hów comelỳ, Puts ìn-vin-cīble, Unìversàl reproach, Shoots ìnvisìble.* It would not be worth while to mention such barbarous distortions, if some of them had not been actually proposed and received by scholars. In face of their authority the student may wish to know how Milton uses these words in other places, and looking up in the concordance all the passages where they occur, I find for *Irresistible*, which seems chosen as a word that enforced its accent, this single line

the lines examined.

(41) Of Union irresistible, mov'd on. *P. L.* vi. 63.

As for *invincible*, the word occurs in five other places and begins the line in every one but the following

(42) Thy temperance, invincible besides. *R.* ii. 408.

Universal occurs in twenty-one other places, and always with its ordinary accent, and again seems as if it was chosen because it could not be misread.

Invisible occurs in all fourteen times. Its position in eleven of these makes any other than its modern accentuation impossible. One of the remaining three is example 37 above; the other two are—

(43) To human sense th' invisible exploits. *P. L.* v. 565.
(44) Things not | reveal'd | which th' in|vísible King. vii. 122.

Both these lines are printed with the elision of *the* in the first edition,[1] which excludes the contraction *invis'ble*, and in example 43 gives *invísible.* No. 44, if it stood alone, would sustain the Chaucerian *invisíble*; but there is no doubt that an inversion of the fourth foot is here intended to enforce the mystery of the sense.

Infinite occurs in all twenty-three times. In twenty-one its common accentuation is necessary; of the other two, one is

(45) Infinite wrauth, and infinite despaire? iv. 74.

which contains an inversion of the first foot, as example 36, which is the other case, does of the second.

It would be difficult to find words the accent of which is better fitted to secure the inversion of the rhythm, or the usage of which in the poem is better established. I have also in one or two cases pointed out the relation which their rhythmical effect bears to the sense. The meaning in 22 and 23 must strike every one. In examples 32, 33 and 34, it seems to introduce a lyrical wave, the contradiction of which to the epic flow of the verse may suggest a remoteness of beauty very like the idea in the words; and we have the very same condition of things in

In the Visions of God. xi. 377.

But, not to say anything which might appear fanciful, I leave this suggestion to the reader, and refer him generally to the chorus on p. 62.

The twelve-syllable line.

The next peculiarity of rhythm which I will take is the twelve-syllable verse, or line with six stresses.

[1] I used the 'facsimile reproduction' of Elliot Stock, 1877, in my first edition, and have in this collated with Beeching's text. Clarendon Press, 1900.

These verses occur in the lyrical parts only of *Samson*: there are some twenty-six in all. It is usually considered that this line (sometimes called an Alexandrine) must have a break or caesura in the middle, between the sixth and seventh syllables. It is best known in this form, and the break is commonly so well marked, that in free unrhymed verse it is indistinguishable from a pair of six-syllable lines. The characteristic of Milton's twelve-syllable line is his neglect of this break, and he makes a verse which has a strong unity in itself, and no tendency to break up. In fact, though he allows himself the same liberty of caesura in this as he does in his ten-syllable verse (see p. 43), yet his 'Alexandrine' is sometimes almost more coherent, as if it was composed expressly to counteract its tendency to divide into two. And here I should think that there was probably another stumbling-block for readers of *Samson*, if it were not for the great popularity of Milton's *Nativity Ode*, where the twelve-syllable lines that close the stanzas are made in the same way, and, with other examples of his early verse, show that he always took the same view of the rhythm of this line. Here are a few well-known lines from the Ode:—

how handled by Milton.

(46) And leave her dolorous mansions to the peering day.
(47) Swindges the scaly Horrour of his folded tail.
(48) The sable-stoled Sorcerers bear his worshipt Ark.
(49) She strikes a universall Peace through Sea and Land.
(50) While Birds of Calm sit brooding on the charmed wave.

In *Samson* about nine of these lines are 6 + 6, with the common break, which is, however, often weak or disguised: four are 7 + 5 (see ex. 71): three are 8 + 4: one is 4 + 5 + 3: one is 5 + 7: one is 5 + 3 + 4: and seven are continuous lines without any break. These, which are characteristic and show the sweep of the rhythm, are here given:

(51) Or grovling soild thir crested helmets in the dust. 141.

(52) To lowest pitch of abject fortune thou art fall'n. 169.
(53) To deaths benumming Opium as my only cure. 630.
(54) Left me all helpless with th' irreparable loss. 644.
(55) And condemnation of the ingrateful multitude. 696.
(56) Seeming at first all heavenly under virgin veil. 1035.
(57) This Idols day hath bin to thee no day of rest. 1297.

This last line might be taken as an example of 4+4+4.

Ambiguity of heavy endings.

It should be remarked on these twelve-syllable lines that some of them may be reduced to ten-syllable lines, by reckoning the last two syllables as extra-metrical (see p. 5).

(58) Made Arms ridiculous, useless the fórgery. 131. (6 + 6.)
(59) Hopeless are all my evils, all remédiless. 648. (7 + 5.)
(60) So deal not with this once thy glorious Cham(pion). 705.
(61) The Image of thy strength, and mighty mínister. 706. (6+6.)

Such an explanation would be quite out of the question if the ten-syllable verse were judged by that of *P. L.*, though a few lines might seem to support it; but in *Samson* Milton has used heavier endings: here are a few,—

(62) Nothing of all these evils hath befáll'n me. 374.
(63) Samson, of all thy sufferings think the héaviest. 445.
(64) Private respects must yield; with grave authórity. 868.
(65) Besides, how vile, contemptible, ridículous. 1361.
(66) No better way I saw then by impórtuning. 797.
(67) Of brazen shield and spear, the hammered cuírass. 132.
(68) Thy son is rather slaying them, that oútcry. 1517.

and thus *thérefore*, *sílence*, *delíverance*, *diminútion*, *submission*, *&c.* The lines last quoted, and ex. 60, must all be taken as ten-syllable lines with extrametrical endings, but it is of no consequence how (58) (59) (61) are explained, although they are almost certainly meant for twelve-syllable verses.

Opening verses of first chorus analysed.

The reader might now take the opening of the first chorus, and see how the various lines which have been already described are put together, and how the verse, with the exception of the lines given on p. 55, is all resolved into disyllabic rising rhythm.

(69) This, this | is he; | sóftly | a while,

an eight-syllable line, with third foot inverted; the sibilants are hushing.

(2) Lét us | nót break | in u|pón him;

a perfect four-foot line in falling rhythm (see p. 55).

(70) O change | beyond | report, | thóught, or | belief!

a ten-syllable line, metre reflective: the fourth foot inverted for wonder.

(71) See how | he lies | at ran|dom, care|lessly | diffus'd,

the first twelve-syllable line in the poem, 7 + 5. In describing great Samson stretched on the bank, it describes itself.

(72) With lang|uish't head | unpropt,

a six-syllable line, its shortness is the want of support.

(73) As one | past hope, | aban-(don'd)
(74) And by | himself | giv*en* o-(ver);

two six-syllable lines, with extrametrical final syllables suggestive of negligence.

(75) In sla|vish ha|b*it*, ill-fit-|ted weeds

an eight-syllable line with elision in third foot: see above, p. 47.

(76) O're worn | and soild;

a four-syllable line; its shortness and simple diction are the poverty of the subject.

(77) Or do | my eyes | misre|present? | Can this | be hee,

a twelve-syllable line (8 + 4); the length of the verse suggests the crowding of new ideas.

(2) Thát He|róick, | thát Re|now'n'd,

a seven-syllable line, the rhythm heralding

(22) Írre|sísti|ble Sam|son? whom | unarm'd,

a ten-syllable line, with first two feet inverted, descriptive of Samson's violence.

(78) No strength | of man, | nor fier|cest wild | beast could | withstand;

a heavy twelve-syllable line, descriptive of Samson's strength.

(79) Who tore | the Li|on, as | the Li|on tears | the Kid,

same with break disguised. Observe how the first half of the line is more powerful than the second.

(80) Ran on | embat|telld Ar|mies clad | in I(ron),

a ten-syllable line, with final extrametrical syllable. The ease of the metre after the two alexandrines is Samson's successful rush.

(81) And wea|ponless | himself,

a six-syllable line; its shortness is Samson's nakedness and singlehandedness.

(58) Made Arms | ridí|cŭloŭs, | úselĕss | thĕ fór|gĕrȳ

a twelve-syllable line, with fourth foot inverted, and weak ending to each half, descriptive of the failure of the preparations.

This will serve for an example. The relation of the form of the verse to the sense is not intended to be taken exactly; it is a matter of feeling between the two, and is misrepresented by any definition. Poetry would be absurd in which there was perpetual verbal mimicry of the sense; but this is not to deny that matter and form should be in live harmonious relation. The above passage happens to be rich in opportunities for descriptive rhythm, and it was necessary to the purpose of this chapter to draw attention to Milton's observation of these, because this often explains what has been censured as harsh or careless irregularity in the verse. Nor have I much indulged my fancy; it will have struck many readers that in the line (ex. 75) where Milton puts his hero in rags he must have been conscious that he was putting his verse into rags; for he always rejected such a garment as he here weaves as unworthy of his Muse.

Examples of free rhythm.

Lastly, I will indicate a few examples of the free rhythms which are carried by the regular disyllabic structure.

Ex. 14 above reads,

> Ín thĕ Ă|rábĭăn | wóods em|bóst.

(82) Príson within Príson | īn|séparably | dárk. 153, 4.

This rhythm made of two six-syllable lines, the first of which has its first and last feet inverted, the second a weak middle foot.

(83) But the heárt | of the Fóol | . 298.

which is also a six-syllable line, with its first two feet inverted, and may be added to examples 20–30 above, p. 56.

(84) With toúch æthérĭăl of Héav'ñ's fíĕrÿ ród. 549.

a ten-syllable line, which reads thus by means of three elisions and one weak place.

(85) My | gríefs nŏt onlÿ | pain mĕ as ă | língring dĭs|eáse. 617–18.

two six-syllable lines, with extrametrical syllable at the end of first, followed by a weak foot and inversion in the second.[1]

(86) Mánÿ ăre thĕ | saÿíngs ŏf thĕ | wíse. 652.

which is an eight-syllable line, with its inverted first foot containing an elision, and with a weak third foot.

(87) Témperst thy | próvidence | thróugh his | shórt cóurse. 670.

thus reads an ordinary ten-syllable line with first and fourth inverted.

(88) Thérefore Gods universal Law. 1053.

[1] This line was misquoted in earlier editions of this tract.

begins a passage of seven short lines, every one of which has the first foot inverted, so that the whole reads as verse in falling rhythm, interspersed with 'dactyls'.

('Idolatry.')

Drúnk with I|dólatry, | drúnk with | Wine. 1670.

This 'dactylic' verse scans thus:

Drúnk with | idól|*a*try, drúnk | with wíne,

with elision in the third foot, see p. 47. The concordance gives eight references for *idolatry*, *idolatrous*, &c., and the word has always its common accentuation; but in the two lines quoted from *Samson* (p. 47, ex. 11, 12) the third syllable is elided or contracted. There can be no doubt of this; but there is a third line, commencing also with two 'dactyls',

(89) By the idolatrous rout amidst their wine. 443.

and, given the contraction of *idolatrous* in the two other places, as Shakespeare has it,

But now he's gone, and my idol*a*trous fancy. *All W.* i. 1.

this would scan most simplý with a common inversion of first foot,

Bý the | idól|*a*trous rout | amidst | their wine.

But in the first edition it is printed with elision of *the*, which gives

Bý th' I|dóla|trous roút | amidst | thir wine,

and puts it among the examples of verses which invert the first two feet. I had before supposed that the elision of *the* was a mistake of the printer or his reader, but this scansion, though further fetched, is more like the rhythm: either is a fiction, and neither contradicts the rhythm.

In recognizing the fictitious 'dactylic' character of some of these lines (compare also the three 'dactyls' in ex. 58), the reader must not believe that true 'dactylic' verse, or verse made of true trisyllabic units, was practically unknown in Milton's time. It was quite common : indeed common is the right term for it, because the greater poets thought it beneath their style. Milton was, therefore, not inventing anything new or unheard, but seeking rather to make a good use of natural English stress rhythms, without falling into their singsong, or setting all his verse to dance. And it should now be clear to the reader by what means he did this.

PART III
ON
OBSOLETE MANNERISMS

¶ *On recession of accent.*

Recession of accent is not now heard. I have been told that it lingers in Ireland in the common speech in which it must have originated, and that Roman Catholics there will still talk of *éxtreme unction*, just as Milton has *éxtreme shift* in *Comus*: also that they do not say Sir Jóhn Róbinson, but Sír-john Róbinson; in the fashion in which, I suppose, our names Sinclair (Silliger) and St. John (Sínjun) arose: which tempts me to quote from Milton's sonnets,

Receſsion

(1) Thy age like ours, O soul of Sir John Cheek.

Ignorance of this old-fashioned habit causes unsuspected misreading of many familiar lines in our poetry. The industry of Dr. Alexander Schmidt put Shakespeare's practice free of conjecture, and the examples that he collected are convincing. The 'rule' is that disyllabic adjectives and participles accented on the last syllable will shift their accent back if they occur before a noun accented on the first syllable.

in Shakespeare.

Dr. Schmidt's remarks are not all pertinent. The facts must be that colliding accents were disliked in common speech and therefore avoided by shifting the accent. This shift must have originated in the commonest phrases (like *extreme unction* above) and have been extended from them; and it would follow that words in this unstable condition would shift their accent under a less provocation than that which first displaced it and also that other occitone disyllables (and especially compounds with like prefix) would

Dr. Schmidt's account of it.

imitate them. The notion that the displacement of the accent is caused by its position in the verse is inadmissible. These words must have first acquired their unusual pronunciation before the poet could have relied on their obeying the verse-stress.

Here are Schmidt's illustrations of Shakespeare's practice :

(2) He is complète in feature and in mind. *Gent.* ii. 4. 73.
(3) Can pierce a *complete* bos(om). Why I desire thee. *Meas.* i. 3. 3.
(4) A maid of grace and *cómplete* majesty. *L.L.L.* i. 1. 137.
(5) Than all the *cómplete* armour that thou wear'st. *Rich.* 3rd, iv. 4. 189.
(6) Though time seem so advèrse and means unfit. *Alls*, v. 1. 26.
(7) Thy *ádverse* party is thy advocate. *Sonn.* 35. 10.
(8) Therefore my verse to constancy confíned. *Sonn.* 105. 7.
(9) Supposed as forfeit to a *cónfined* doom. *Sonn.* 107. 4.
(10) Have you conspired, have you with these contríved. *Mid.* iii. 2. 196.
(11) To do no *cóntrived* murd(er): I lack iniquity. *Oth.* i. 2. 3.
(12) So then I am not lame, poor, nor despísed. *Sonn.* 37. 9.
(13) The pangs of *déspised* love, the laws delay. *Ham.* iii. 1. 72.
(14) And not the puddle in thy sea dispérsed. *Lucr.* 658.
(15) The *díspersed* air, who, holding Lucrece' life. *Lucr.* 1805.
(16) And make distínct the very breach, whereout. *Tro.* iv. 5. 245.
(17) To offend, and judge, are *dístinct* offices. *Mer.* ii. 9. 61.
(18) With *dístinct* breath and *cónsigned* kisses to them. *Tro.* iv. 4. 47.
(19) This fellow is distráct and so am I. *Err.* iv. 3. 42.
(20) Their *dístract* parcels in combined sums. *Compl.* 231 (? author).
(21) O royal knavery! an exáct command. *Ham.* v. 2. 19.
(22) To set the *éxact* wealth of all our states. 1st *Hen.* 4th, iv. 1. 46.
(23) I have with *éxact* view perused thee, Hector. *Tro.* iv. 5. 232.
(24) Let their exháled unwholesome breaths make sick. *Lucr.* 779.
(25) And be no more an *éxhaled* meteor. 1st *Hen.* 4th, v. 1. 19.
(26) To work my mind, when body's work 's expíred. *Sonn.* 27. 4.
(27) An *éxpired* date, cancelled ere well begun. *Lucr.* 26.
(28) To the contrary I have exprèss commandment. *Wint.* ii. 2. 8.

(29) As bid me tell my tale in *éxpress* words. *John* iv. 2. 234.
(30) Savage, extréme, rude, cruel, not to trust. *Sonn.* 129. 4.
(31) And *éxtreme* fear can neither fight nor fly. *Lucr.* 230.
(32) But qualify the fïre's *éxtreme* rage. *Gent.* ii. 7. 22.
(33) The *éxtreme* parts of time extremely forms.
L. L. L. v. 2. 750.
(34) Tempering extremities with *éxtreme* sweet.
Rom. ii. *Prolog.*
(35) To some forlórn and naked hermitage. *L. L. L.* v. 2. 805.
(36) And from the *fórlorn* world his visage hide. *Sonn.* 33. 7.
(37) Round rising hillocks, brakes obscúre and rough. *Ven.* 237.
(38) His means of death, his *óbscure* funeral. *Ham.* iv. 5. 213.
(39) In so profoúnd abysm I throw all care. *Sonn.* 112. 9.
(40) There 's matter in these sighs, these *prófound* heaves.
Ham. iv. 1. 1.
(41) Open the door, secúre, fool-hardy king. *R.* 2nd, v. 3. 43.
(42) Upon my *sécure* hour thy uncle stole. *Ham.* i. 5. 61.
(43) To lip a wanton in a *sécure* couch. *Oth.* iv. 1. 72.
(44) Which knows no pity, but is still sevére. *Ven.* 1000.
(45) And let go by the ac(tor). O just but *sévere* law.
Meas. ii. 2. 41.
(46) His love sincére, his thoughts immaculate. *Gent.* ii. 7. 76.
(47) Sir, in good sooth, in *síncere* verity. *Lear*, ii. 2. 111.
(48) Neither supréme, how soon confusion. *Cor.* iii. 1. 110.
(49) The life of purity, the *súpreme* fair. *Lucr.* 780.
(50) But as we, under heaven, are *súpreme* head. *John* iii. 1. 155.

He also draws instances from the doubtful plays of *bénign*, *córrupt*, *rémiss*; and brings under his rule the well-known instances of *exiled* and *humane*; (which we may here dismiss, for Milton's *exil'd* never collides, and he distinguishes *human* and *humane* as we do though not always in the spelling ;) he also quotes

(51) Have you done yet? Alack our *térrene* moon.
Ant. iii. 13. 153.

to which may be added

(52) Open their *cóngealed* mouths and bleed afresh.
Rich. 3rd, i. 2. 56.
(53) My *cóncealed* lady to our cancelled love. *Rom.* iii. 3. 98.
(54) Of murderous lech(ers): and in the *máture* time.
Lear, iv. 6. 282.

Schmidt concludes his essay with instancing the similarly shifting accent of disyllables compounded of *un*, as *unbacked*, *unbid*, *unblown*, *unborn*, *unbound*, *unchaste*, *&c.* (and I should class with these the compounds of *mis-*), which may be considered as parallel cases; but these disyllables are made up of a positive and a negative syllable, both of which carry some stress in ordinary speech, with either one or other insisted on according to the sense of the speaker; and they may thus easily take either accent in verse, and they differ in this from such words as *divine*, *secure*, *profound*, *&c.*, which are, or have become, irresoluble units with one single well-marked stress. I, therefore, class these apart, and shall consider them separately.

This being the Shakespearian tradition we must determine whether it is the explanation of any of the verse-rhythms in *P. L.* There is no doubt that cases of recession of accent occur in Milton's early poems:

used in Milton's earlier poems.

(55) About the *súpreme* Throne. *Time*, 17.
(56) In Regions mild of calm and *sérene* Ayr. *Com.* 4.
(57) And he, the *Súpreme* good, t' whom all things ill. 217.
(58) Not any boast of skill, but *éxtreme* shift. 272.
(59) She, that hath that, is clad in *cómpleat* steel. 421.
(60) Wherwith she freezed her foes to *cóngeal'd* stone. 449.
(61) The *dívine* property of her first being. 469.
(62) The *súblime* notion, and high mystery. 785.

I should say that the above are all genuine cases; and yet most of these verses, if they occurred in *P. L.* (and a few similar ones do occur), I should explain differently.

obviates a common irregu-larity.

The matter stands thus: in all Milton's verse there is a frequent occurrence of the following rhythm, that is, a foot of two unstressed short syllables preceding a foot composed of two heavy syllables, as in these lines from Shakespeare's *Midsummer-Night's Dream*,

(63) The ploughman lost his sweat, ănd thĕ grēēn cōrn.
(64) Before milkwhite, now purplĕ wĭth lōvē's wōund.
(65) Love takes the meanĭng ĭn lōvē's cōnference.

It is common in Milton's early verse, which is much influenced by the verse of Shakespeare's first style; and he always made use of it. Whatever the account may be, it is pleasant to the ear in the smoothest verse, and is so, no doubt, by a kind of compensation in it. In typical cases there is no possibility of stress in the first short foot, and the first heavy syllable of the next foot seems to carry what has been omitted, with an accentuation bearing relation to the sense. Instances occur everywhere in Milton.

It will readily be seen that this is a condition of things which must very often do away with the necessity for supposing recession of accent; for if a passage occurs in which recession of accent might be supposed, it is merely in this usual condition of rhythm, and may be in order without it: and further, the more the verse frees itself, by assertion of stress, from the common smooth flow of alternate accents, and exhibits variety of rhythm, as Milton's late verse does, the more will the ear allow this, or any other recognized irregularity to intrude itself without support from the sense; and the less will it be prepared or disposed to correct such weak places by the conventional metric stress: or, to put the same thing in another way, there is a very strong reason why Milton should have excluded the licence of recession of accent from *P. L.*; because the uncertainty which it introduces as to whether a syllable should be stressed or not, and the tendency which it has to make the verse smooth at all cost, would infect his inversions with uncertainty, and on these the character of his rhythm in a great measure depended. If we add to this consideration the rarity of possible instances in all *Paradise Lost*, *Regained*, and *Samson*,—putting the question of prepositions aside—the evidence that Milton did actually intend to renounce this licence is very convincing. I have noted only these:

excluded from *P.L.*

doubtful examples considered.

(66) Next Chemos, th' óbscene dread of Moabs sons. i. 406.
(67) And sat as Princes, whom the súpreme King. i. 735.

A doubtful example, for with the same sense we have the same rhythm as *supréme* would make, in *P. L.* i. 40, &c.

(68) Encamp their Legions; or with óbscure wing. ii. 132.
(69) Our Súpream Foe in time may much remit. ii. 210.

this may be a common inversion of first foot.

(70) In cónfus'd march forlorn, th' adventurous Bands. ii. 615.

the suggestion of confusion here is surely better in the rhythm than in the pronunciation.

(71) Through the pure marble Air his oblique way. iii. 564.

The words *complete*, *extreme*, *serene*, *sublime*, together occur in all twenty-four times in *Paradise Lost*, *Paradise Regained*, and *Samson*, and are always accented on the last. Each of these words occurs once in *Comus*, and there suffers recession of accent (see exx. above 55 et seq.): and it is worth observing that in *P. L.*, *divine Sémblance*, ix. 606, and *supréme Kingdom*, vi. 814, are divided between two lines.

The word *adverse* cannot be reckoned, for though Milton uses both accents, the choice seems arbitrary (see ii. 77): and we still accent the word either way. It is like the adjectives compounded with *un*; and of these I have remarked only *unknown* as being in a double condition.

(72) Or *únknown* Region, what remains him less
Then *únknown* dangers. ii. 443, 4.

Uncouth is always accented on the first: and for *prostrate*, which might seem from the line quoted on p. 42 to have a shifting accent, see the remarks there.

If the reader will now observe that all the six examples (seven if *únknown* be counted,) of recession or doubtful recession occur in the first three books of *P. L.*, he will, I think, agree that Milton purposely excluded recession from *P. L.*, as he did extra-metrical syllables within the line, for fear of introducing uncertainty into his rhythms, but that the necessity of avoiding it altogether was not at first fully realized, or that his old habit was not quite conquered. The only fallacy here must lie in the premises, and it is possible enough that I may have overlooked some examples.

Disyllabic prepositions.

I cannot think that this habit of avoiding colliding accents was entirely confined to adjectives and participles, it is most probable that similar occitone disyllables that caused the same inconvenience would obviate it in the same way, and it is for this reason that we find the prepositions *withoút*, *beyońd*, *amońg*, *befoŕe*, *unléss*, *whereón*, *wheŕeby*, and perhaps others, in an uncertain condition.

'without.'

Of these words I think it is convenient and justifiable to consider *without* as an exception, and regard it frankly as a word of indeterminate accent. The fact is that in its presumably original form accented on the last syllable it is a powerful word, very suitable where the sentence makes its enforcement desirable, but much too heavy for common use. It is unfortunate that we have not besides it some light monosyllable for the negation of *with*—a word like *nith* would be a great boon. Shakespeare experimented with *sans*, but not wholeheartedly enough to establish it ; he probably felt it to be unsatisfactory, and shared the popular instinct which has refused it. The concordance gives only these examples :

(73) *Holofernes.* I do sans question. *L. L. L.* v. 1. 91.

(74) And when *Biron* says 'My love to thee is sound, sans crack or flaw', *Rosaline* replies, 'Sans sans, I pray you'. v. 2. 415.

(75) *Jacques.* And I did laugh sans intermission. *A. Y. L.* ii. 7. 32.

(76) Sans teeth, sans eyes, sans taste, sans everything. 166.

(77) *Dromio.* Sans fable, she herself reviled you there. *Com. E.* iv. 4. 76.

(78) *Bastard.* Come, come; sans compliment, what news abroad?
K. J. v. 6. 16.
(79) *Ulysses.* Sans check to good and bad. *T. & C.* i. 111. 94.
(80) *Timon.* Sans remorse. *T. of A.* iv. 3. 122.
(81) *Brabantio.* Nature . . . sans witchcraft could not.
Othell. i. 3. 64.
(82) *Ham.* Ears without hands or eyes, smelling sans all.
Ham. iii. 4. 97.
(83) *Prosp.* A confidence sans bound. *Temp.* i. 2. 79.

The word is ridiculed in *L. L. L.* and is somewhat self-conscious in all but the latest examples, where it is used honestly.

Milton rejected *sans*, and if we are reduced to *withoút*, it is impossible to recognize its extravagant phonetic pretensions, for they are so great as often to out-face the sonority of the main word of the sentence and thus disfigure the sense. In the following examples No. 85 from his early work seems a plain instance of full recession. No. 103, which shows a full accent on the last, seems to carry most of the others with it. But a third condition of the word is possible, in which neither syllable should be enforced, and this seems indicated by No. 102.

Since in doubtful cases preference must be influenced by habit, and we cannot be sure of Milton's habit, our judgement must be suspended:

(84) The brood of folly *without* father bred. *Pens.* 2.
(85) Here be *without* duck or nod. *Com.* 960.
(86) That comes to all; but torture *without* end. *P. L.* i. 67.
(87) Must exercise us *without* hope of end. ii. 89.
(88) Illimitable Ocean *without* bound. ii. 892.
(89) Loud as from numbers *without* number, sweet. iii. 346.
(90) In whose conspicuous count'nance, *without* cloud. iii. 385.
(91) He views in bredth, and, *without* longer pause. iii. 561.
(92) Him first, him last, him midst and *without* end. v. 165.
(93) One Kingdom, Joy and Union *without* end. vii. 161.
(94) Varietie *without* end; but of the Tree. vii. 542.
(95) Smooth sliding *without* step, last led me up. viii. 302.
(96) Us happie, and *without* Love no happiness. viii. 621.
(97) And forty days Eliah, *without* food. *P. R.* i. 353.
(98) From National obstriction, *without* taint. *Sam.* 312.

(99) Alone, and *withoút* gúide, half lost, I seek. *P. L.* ii. 975.
(100) Love *without* end, and *withóut* méasure Grace. iii. 142.
(101) Flours of all hue, and *withoút* Thórn the Rose. iv. 256.
(102) In mystic Dance nót *withóut* Sóng, resound. v. 178.
(103) Ordaind withoút redemption, *withoút* end. v. 615.

Of the other words in this class the following lines are examples :

other prepositions

(104) Thir seasons: *among* these the seat of men. *P. L.* vii. 623.
(105) And not molest us, *uńless* we our selves. viii. 186.
(106) Still glorious *before* whom awake I stood. 464.
(107) The Stairs were such as *whéreon* Jacob saw. iii. 510.
(108) From the Asian kings and Parthian *among* these.
P. R. iv. 73.
(109) And be thy self Man *among* men on Earth. *P. L.* iii. 283.
(110) Thy goodness *beyond* thought, and Power Divine. v. 159.
(111) Successful *beyond* hope, to lead ye forth. x. 463.
(112) Wisdom without their leave? and *wherein* lies. ix. 725.
(113) This dreaded time have compast, *wherein* we. *P. R.* i. 58.
(114) And Country *whéreof* here needs no account.
P. L. iv. 235.
(115) Winnows the buxom Air; till *within* soare. v. 270.
(116) Of knowledge *within* bounds; beyond abstain. vii. 120.
(117) By Prophet or by Angel, *unless* thou. *P. R.* iii. 352.

The above quotations will show the rarer exceptional conditions of these words. Of these No. 105 requires recession, and explains 117. Nos. 107 and 114 seem to me cases of recession.

The liberty allowed in the accentuation of these words was traditional ; for example Shakespeare has,

(118) That *théreby* beauty's rose might never die. Sonnet i. 2.
(119) Who if it wink, shall *théreon* fall and die. Lucr. 1139.
(120) All ignorant that soul that sees thee *wíthout* wonder.
L. L. L. iv. 2. 117.
(121) Can you still dream and pore and *théreon* look. iv. 3. 298.

If these words are accented at all they must be a cause of uncertainty in the rhythm. The solution seems to be that they can be pronounced without any speech accent at all : and if this be accepted, the collection of instance which go to prove it will not have been useless.

probably lose their accent.

Recession used by later poets.

But even if Milton, as I suppose, wished to banish recession of accent from his later prosody, it did not disappear from English poetry. There are strangely many examples of it in Shelley, in whose verse it is generally unrecognized. The extremely beautiful and delicate inventions which he contributed to the rhythms of blank verse are, I think, generally lacking in the quality which critics call roughness in Milton, and readily betray irregularities which are uncongenial to them. Thus in the *Witch of Atlas* in the following line,

> A haven, béneath whose translucent floor. xlix.

beneath was, I suppose, sounded *bènneath*, but possibly, as we read it now, without any accent at all.

The word *serene*, which Shelley usually stressed as we do, removes its accent away to the first syllable, when followed by a contiguous stress.

> Or sérene morning air; and far beyond. *Epips.* 438.
> Through which his soul, like Vesper's sérene beam.
> *Athan.* i. 61.
> And profoundest midnight shroud the sérene lights of heaven.

There is an example of recession in the first stanza of *The Skylark*,

> In prófuse strains of unpremeditated art.

the word *divine* is in the same condition,

> And lofty hopes of dívine liberty. *Alastor*, 159.
> Bore to thy honour through the dívine gloom. *Prom.* iii. 3.
> The herd went wandering o'er the dívine mead.
> *Hymn-Merc.* lxxxvi.

And thus *intense*, *distinct*, *supreme*, *extreme*:

> By sightless lightning?—th' íntense atom glows. *Ad.* xx.
> The dístinct valley and the vacant woods. *Alast.* 195.
> God is one súpreme goodness, one pure essence.
> *Cald.* i. 115, &c.
> Thy éxtreme hope, the loveliest and the last. *Ad.* vi.

> His éxtreme way to her dim dwellingplace. *Ad.* viii.
> Scarce visible from éxtreme loveliness. *Epips.* 104, &c.

Thus also *antique*, and *obscene*.

The new Concordance to Shelley's poems, by Mr. F. S. Ellis, published in 1892 by Mr. Quaritch, will give ample evidence of Shelley's practice: I observe in it that the line

> Its stony jaws: the abrupt mountain breaks. *Alast.* 551.

is given with *abrupt* accented on the first syllable. The line with the usual accentuation has a fine Miltonic rhythm, in correspondence with the sense; and it is an interesting confirmation of what I said above of the character of Shelley's rhythms, that the compiler of the dictionary, whose acquaintance with Shelley's verse must be of a most exceptional kind, should have considered that rhythm impossible.

ℭ *Spelling.*

Milton's spelling peculiar

The spelling in the original edition of *P. L.* is peculiar, and its peculiarities are intentional and betray their purpose: it is, therefore, regrettable that later editors disregarded and, by conforming the text to the current standard, withheld from Milton's readers the assistance that he had thought well to provide for them. I am glad to have been myself the exciting cause of the late Dean Beeching's scholarly edition, made in Yattendon for the Clarendon Press in 1899, which is now in every one's hands and saves me from any obligation of describing the spelling, further than the purpose of the prosody requires, and this has been already done, though a few general remarks may here be added.

I had myself been familiar only with the common texts, and wrote from my knowledge of them: but before printing my tract I had read the poem through in a facsimile of the first edition, and came to the following conclusions.

First, that—excluding words, the spelling of which is fanciful or antique, such as *highth* for *height*, and *thir* for *their*—the spelling is phonetic in intention, its object being to ensure the verse being read rightly. For instance, when a line has more than ten syllables, if there is any doubt about the place of the elision, it is shown by an apostroph. Again a distinction is made between the enclitic and emphatic pronoun *me*, which in some places is spelt *mee*.

and inconsistent.

The facts are sufficiently summarized in Dean Beeching's preface; and he shows that the spelling is not consistent; e.g. that the mark of elision is often missing where it would seem to be required, and that the distinctive spelling of *me* is not always observed, and in some cases seems to be wrong.

No doubt this inconsistency was one reason why careful scholars refused to perpetuate the text; for unless they were satisfied that their duty was to transmit faithfully what Milton actually left, mistakes and all, their only choice was either to perpetuate what they judged to be errors, or to take the responsibility of regulating peculiarities, the object of which they did not fully understand.

It is not to be wondered that errors exist in Milton's text; the wonder is that, being blind, he was able to contrive so accurate a text of his long poem; he must have exercised incredible patience; and if he consider'd, as he must have done, that without the use of his eyes he could never ensure perfect accuracy, he would then have rightly judged that, provided he exposed his intention sufficiently, many inconsistencies were better than a few; since, the fewer they were, the more likely would they be to pass for true instructions, whereas by an evident laxity he would escape perverse misinterpretation.

inconsistency intentional.

He would then have insisted on the phonetic peculiarities of his spelling in some typical and in all exceptional doubtful or difficult places, and have been willing to leave the rest to the instinct or habit of his amanuensis and printer. And the spelling looks to me as if it were in that purposely lax and accidental condition.

A tabulation of all the exceptions might, perhaps, settle the questions here raised, but I have not myself undertaken that labour.

¶ *Pronunciation.*

Milton's pronunciation much like ours.

In the first edition of this book I disregarded this whole subject except parenthetically because I was of opinion that the pronunciation in Milton's time did not so differ from our own as to need general attention in an examination of his verse.

prepositions.

But I was led to adopt the suggestion that the monosyllabic prepositions, *to*, *from*, *with*, &c., might have had more stress value in Milton's time than they have now. I do not see any sign of this in Milton's verse, and I would not have raised the doubt if the following disproof had occurred to me. Shakespeare, whose early verse may be described as syllabic, came to write a verse more and more dependent on stress, which we may assume was the speech-accent of his time ; and from his later work we can judge of the relative stress-values of the syllables in the sentences. Now the prepositions in question are among the first words to refuse accentual place : in the following passage from *Antony and Cleopatra* observe how comfortable the italicized prepositions are before and after a peculiarly weak syllabic line of three accents,

> We must retúrn *to the* court of guard : the night
> Is shiny ; and, they say, we shall embattle
> *By the* sécond hoúr, *in the* morn.

It would appear from such verse as this that these prepositions had even less syllabic value in the speech of Shakespeare's time than they have now ; and I suppose it follows that they had not more in Milton's time.

Experts exaggerate differences.

It has seemed to me as if it was the fashion of the present day rather to exaggerate the difference between the older pronunciation and our own. With regard to *r* it is, I believe, universally assumed that it was without exception trilled throughout England in Chaucer's time. But in Freeman's *Norman Conquest*, vol. ii, p. 511 of the third edition under his account of Westminster Abbey, which was at first called Thorney Abbey, is the following note :

(Trilled *r*.)

'Wace (10653) enlarges on the name, and his phonetic spelling illustrates his natural difficulty in pronouncing the letter þ.

> En un islet esteit assise,
> *Zonée* out nom, joste Tamise ;
> *Zonée* por ço l'apelon,
> Ke d'espine i out foison,
> E ke l'ewe en alout environ.
> *Ee* en engleiz isle apelon,
> *Ee* est isle, *zon* est espine,
> Seit rainz, seit arbre, seit racine ;
> *Zonée*, ço est en engleiz
> Isle d'espine en franceiz.'

But if Zonee has lost its 'thorn' it has lost also its trilled *r*, and is written exactly as a Frenchman would to-day transliterate our present pronunciation of *thorny*, from which it seems to me to follow that *thorn* was pronounced in London in the twelfth century without trill as it is now : for if the *r* had been trilled it would surely have appeared in the Norman-French as *zorn*. There may, perhaps, be some other explanation of this.

('one')

Again I find experts all agreed that the word *one* was pronounced in Shakespeare's time as we pronounce *own*. But in Tyndall's Gospels (1526) this word is most frequently spelt *won*. Both spellings *one* and *won* occur: and this positive evidence for a recognized pronunciation *won* is complete seventy years before Shakespeare.

Old-fashioned accentuation of certain words.

It is true that a number of words are to be found in Milton's poems which he stresses differently from us; and these are generally marked with their peculiar accent in the common editions. The following list of them was taken from Nares's *Orthoepy*; I do not know how complete it is, and I have omitted a few words, which I thought doubtful or not requiring notice.

Aspéct. Áttribúted (Nares is not justified by *P. R.* iii. 69. in asserting an alternative Attríbuted). Blasphémous. Brígad. Captíve (verb). Colleágue. Commércing. Comráde. Consúlt (subst.). Contést (subst.). Cóntribute. Converse (subst.). Convóy (subst.). Crystállin. Egréss. Exíle. Fárewell. Impúlse. Instínct (subst.). Midníght. Perfúme (subst.). Precíncts. Prescrípt. Procéss. Procínct. Prodúct. Réceptacle. Reflúx. Remédiless. Sepúlchred. Sunbeám. Sunshíne. Survéy (subst.). Travérse (verb). Triúmph (verb, also tríumph). Úncouth. Upróar. Volúbil.[1]

Of the above words, which it will be seen are mostly Latin, a few are peculiar or of very rare occurrence in poetry. The rest of them are either words which were thus accentuated in Milton's time, or words the accent of which had already shifted or was then shifting, and for which he preferred the older or more classical pronunciation. Some of them he himself accents differently in different places: they seldom give rise to any difficulty; and when they do, a knowledge of his rhythms is necessary to solve it.

[1] Some detailed remarks on Nares's list will be found in note J

Knowledge of poet's rhythm necessary.

For if the old poets are to be our authority for the accent and pronunciation of their time, we must first understand their rhythmical intention, nor can trustworthy conclusions be drawn from their verse until the verse be understood; and Milton wrote much more carefully than he has been criticized. The learned Tyrwhitt, for example—to whom I gladly record a heavy debt of enjoyment for his edition of Chaucer,—when commenting on the following verse from the *Prologue* to the *Canterbury Tales*,

Tyrwhitt.

> Of Engelond to Can|ter bú|ry they wénde,

which he thus divides, and arguing against the supposition that Chaucer can have written 'without any restraint' of metrical rule with respect to 'superflous syllables', justly parallels Chaucer's trisyllabic feet with examples from Milton; and, among some lines from *Paradise Lost*, which he explains more or less correctly, he gives our ex. 44, p. 59,

> Things not revealed which the invi|sible King,

which he thus divides, neglecting the 'elision' printed by Milton, and thus giving to the line a wrong rhythm which makes it like his wrong interpretation of the line quoted from Chaucer.

An example of expert pedantry.

That same line of Chaucer may serve me to justify my complaint of what I called the exaggeration of the differences of the old pronunciation. It is one of three lines in the first thirty of the *Prologue* which contain the word Canterbury, and Canterbury is used to fill either three or four places in the verse: thus—

> Of Engelond to Canterbury they wende.
> That toward Canterbury wolden ryde.

from which I should conclude that *Canterbury* was pronounced in Chaucer's time very much as it is now; for we say either *Canterbury* or *Canterb'ry*. But on p. 264 of vol. i of the Aldine edition, I am instructed to pronounce the lines thus—

Of Engelond to Kan'terber'ee dhahy wendë.
Dhat tohwerd Kan'terber'ee wolden reedë.

Whereas thus written, the first of these verses will not scan: and this *ee* of *Canterberee* seems to be at least an exaggeration. It must be the vowel sound of *feel*, Ellis's ii, (the longest of all the i, y, sounds; being twice the i in the French *fini*,) and it is put here for his *ii*, (which is the prolonged or double form of the short *i* in the English *finny*,) presumably for the reason that this latter sound is more difficult of pronunciation, and the instructions are intended for ordinary readers. But even this *ii* would be an extreme allowance of length. It happens that *bury* is one of the words in the table which Ellis gives to illustrate the changes of pronunciation since the fourteenth century, and he writes it ber·*i*, unchanged from Chaucer's time to our own. So that it seems that (ee = ii) the heaviest of all the four i, y, sounds, is put instead of (*i*) the lightest, to show us how to pronounce y, which we should have pronounced correctly if left to ourselves; whereas the antiquary's explanation destroys the verse.

And that unseemly *Dhahy* is just the same sort of futile embarrassment. I imagine that we still pronounce *they* just as Chaucer did, and any modern reader would pronounce the word as he should, if he were left to himself. But who ever did or could pronounce *Dhahy*? The only certainty about it is that it is prolifically suggestive of error.

My purpose in writing these notes on Milton was to draw attention to his workmanship, and on the evidence of his prosody ensure that his verse should be read rightly. It is a common opinion that there is no such thing as English prosody; and most of our classical scholars have regarded the ten-syllable verses of Chaucer, Shakespeare, and Milton, as so many better or worse attempts to compose regular, alternately stressed, so-called iambic lines, broken here and there by the negligent admission of 'superflous' syllables. The language of Tyrwhitt in the following note is typical: he is speaking of rhymed verse:

Tyr-whitt's avowal.

'It is agreed, I believe, that in our heroick metre those verses (considered singly) are the most harmonious in which the accents fall upon the even syllables; but it has never (that I know) been defined how far a verse may vary from this its most perfect form, and yet remain a verse. On the *tenth* (or rhyming) syllable a strong accent is in all cases indispensably required (!), and in order to make the line tolerably harmonious, it seems necessary that at least *two more* of the *even* syllables should be accented, the *fourth* being (almost always) one of them. Milton, however, has not subjected his verse EVEN TO THESE RULES; particularly (either by NEGLIGENCE or design) he has frequently put an unaccented syllable in the *fourth* place.'

Tyrwhitt was a highly gifted scholar with a fine ear for verse. If he was the green tree, what of the dry? In the above quotation from him there is much to find fault with, but buried away in these sentences lies, I believe, the hidden key to the rhythmical rationale of blank verse.

PART IV

ON THE PROSODY OF ACCENTUAL VERSE

Origin of accentual classical verse.

In both the quantitive and syllabic systems of verse there were strict syllabic rules which gave the metre, while the accentual speech-rhythms which overlaid the metre were secondary and superimposed at the taste of the poet. They were like the flesh on a skeleton, and it was one advantage of this system that the skeleton gave free play to the flesh. But these speech-rhythms, whether they enforced or contradicted the fundamental rhythm of the metre, constituted in their variety the main beauty of the versification; and since it must have been for rhythm's sake that the metres were originally invented, their rhythms however elaborated, were their effective quality; so that when the tradition of the prosody was lost, it was natural for versifiers to fall back on the most familiar speech-rhythms of the old verse; even where those were contradictory to the original regular accent of the metre. They did not consciously imagine and remake the old *metre* on an accentual scheme: the gentleman who wrote the line

old rhythms imitated

> Turcos oppressi et barbaras gentes excussi,

while in the second half of his would-be hexameter, he relies somewhat too confidently on the speech-stress to make a 'strawberry jampot' of his amazing false quantities, has in the first half used it to imitate the Virgilian effect of the *un*accentual caesura. And so in these ecclesiastical iambics,

in early hymns.

> Nos tibi reos statuat.
> Christe qui lux es et dies.

the first line accentuates its false quantities quite

their accents not always metrical.

regularly, but the second imitates the old 'unaccentual' inversion of the first foot, common in quantitive writing.

Here are two full stanzas of that hymn :

> Christe qui lux es et dies,
> Noctis tenebras detegis,
> Lucisque lumen crederis
> Lumen beatum praedicans.
>
> Ne gravis somnus irruat,
> Nec hostis nos surripiat,
> Nec caro illi consentiens
> Nos tibi reos statuat.

The famous *Ad Coenam Agni* has these stanzas,

> Ad coenam Agni providi
> Et stolis albis candidi,
> Post transitum maris rubri
> Christo canamus principi.
>
> O vere digna hostia,
> Per quam fracta sunt Tartara,
> Redemta plebs captivata
> Reddita vitae praemia.

Both these hymns are ascribed to the seventh or eighth century.

Rhythms imitated without prosody

A great deal of English verse has been written much in this way. Writers familiar with the poetry have imitated its rhythms without attention to the prosody that originally provoked and sustained them, and their poems give the flesh without any skeleton. A question arises whether this practice is not sound in principle ; whether, if the speech-rhythm be the beauty of the verse, it may not be a sufficient rule for it ; whether indeed, the rhythms of *Par. Lost*, and *Samson*, or even of Dante's *Commedia*, are any the better for their strict syllabic scheme and prosodial fictions.

a legitimate basis ?

Theoretically the problem is this, whether in poetry the speech as determined by its accent and rhythm can be made so persistently beautiful in form as to dispense with all the subtle assistance which it derives from interplay with a fundamental metrical form, which never relaxing its conscious guidance gives special significance to every deviation from it, and overriding all irregularities blends them into a consistent whole; or whether, in renouncing this it must not, if it should do well, create a prosody of its own?

There is nothing to forbid experiment, but it is evident that if we make it, we must not trifle with the conditions, nor supplement and pad out our accentual rhythms with familiar *un*accentual effects borrowed from the prosodies that we have discarded (see note K.)

Coleridge's theory and practice

I shall attempt in this chapter to show what sort of rules this accentual or stress-verse spontaneously develops in practice, and it will be convenient to take Coleridge's *Christabel* for text. He wrote in his preface to that poem, that the metre of it is 'founded on a *new principle*, namely, that of counting in each line the accents, not the syllables. Though the latter may vary from seven to twelve, yet in each line the accents will be found to be only four. Nevertheless this occasional variation in number of syllables is not introduced wantonly, or for the mere ends of convenience, but in correspondence with some transition in the nature of the imagery or passion.'

Here we have the primary rule stated viz., THAT THE METRE IS DETERMINED BY THE NUMBER OF STRESSES OR ACCENTS IN THE LINE.

If we take the first five lines of the poem

> Tis the míddle of níght by the cástle clóck
> And the ówls have awáken'd the crówing cóck,
> Tu—whít!—Tu—whóo!
> And hárk agáin! the crówing cóck
> How drówsilỳ it créw.

we find, neglecting the ambiguous third line, which

seems to have but two accents,[1] the fifth is also deficient. In stress-verse this line can have only two accents thus

How drówsily it créw

but judging by other lines in the poem, it was almost certainly intended to have three, and if so, the second of these is a conventional accent; it does not occur in the speech but in the metre, and has to be imagined because the metre suggests or requires it; and it is plain that if the stress is to be the rule of the metre, the metre cannot be called on to provide the stress.

To save the reader the trouble of turning to the poem to satisfy himself on this point, I will quote some more lines which offend against this law of stressed verse.

Fròm her kénnel benéath the róck,
She máketh ánswer tò the clóck.
À fúrlong fròm the cástle gáte.
Òf her ówn betróthed kníght.

inconsistent.

This poem with its preface has no doubt done much to hinder the right understanding of stressed verse: for Coleridge would not be lightly suspected of thus mistaking his own method:—but it is plain that he did not ever shake off the tradition of these conventional, metric stresses, nor really imagine a stressed verse which should be entirely free from them. The reader will understand that I am not saying that the lines in question are bad or good: they are agreeable enough to the reader for this reason, that the stress not being really creative of the rhythm, but only accenting the regular beats of a loose metre,—an unbroken succession of strong stresses would make

[1] Coleridge's words 'only four accents' can be strained to mean 'not more than four'; but there can be little doubt that *only* refers to the greater number of syllables, and that the intention was to have always four stresses.

monotony or singsong; which is generally avoided throughout *Christabel* by the common methods, the stresses being frequently disregarded, and sometimes overloaded: whereas in pure stressed verse the monotony would be avoided by inverting some of the stresses or leaving them bare, in such a manner as we are led to expect early in the poem by the lines—

> Iś the níght chílly and dárk?
> The níght is chílly, but nót dárk.

With regard to stress *Christabel* is, with such rare exceptions, in the same condition as *L'Allegro*; while the syllabic liberty, so far from being new, is found in English verse from the earliest times.

In the edition of this book which appeared in 1901 I wrote what I believe was the first attempt to make a prosody of English accentual verse as distinct from syllabic verse. I shall reproduce it here with a few omissions and verbal corrections.

¶ ON THE RULES OF THE COMMON LIGHTER STRESS-RHYTHMS, AND OF THE ENGLISH ACCENTUAL HEXAMETER.

Appeal to the ear.

These 'laws' are merely the tabulation of what my ear finds in English stressed or accentual verse: but they appeal confidently to the reader's ear for confirmation. I shall deal with only the lighter forms of these rhythms, that is with such as are commonly called dactylic, anapaestic, comic iambic, and hexameter—so far as stress governs disyllabic metres, it is, I think, sufficiently covered by our examination of Milton—and when I say that anything is not allowable I mean only that it seems to my ear unsatisfactory in these lighter rhythms. *There is no limit to rhythm*, nor can I imagine any kind of effect, or any possible collocation of syllables in a 'foot', which might not be well employed in some poetic metre or other.

Symbols and terms.

I use the symbol ∧ to denote a stressed syllable. This does not imply that it is a long syllable. The properer symbol is an acute accent, single or double; but I do not use that because it is convenient for primary analysis to have a symbol which does not raise the distinction between single and double stress;[1] Again, because the acute accent does not range well with the quantitive symbols – and ◡. It has the appearance of being less important, and thus misrepresents the real units to the eye; the laws moreover to which attention is called are *nova praecepta*, and it is well to have a new symbol to indicate them.

Also I shall use the terms *heavy*, *light*, and *short* to denote the quantitive value of syllables, instead of the usual terms *long* and *short*,[2] for the following reasons:—

classical long and short.

The term *long*, as employed in Greek and Latin prosody, includes not only those syllables which have a long vowel, but also those syllables which have a short vowel long 'by position', that is, having two or more consonants following it; while the term *short* includes only those syllables which have their short

[1] Double stress and the rhythms which it introduces are alluded to below, see p. 103.

[2] Though this true distinction between light and short is not made in the earlier part of this book. I do not find anything there which need cause confusion. On page 70 the sign ◡◡ is used merely to distinguish the *weak feet*: and on pages 63 and 64 to show the light (not always short) places in the dactylic passages of *Samson*. In Milton's blank verse the distinction between light and short (indeed even between light and heavy) implies greater refinement of analysis than is possible in an account of the structure of the verse; and it is open to much uncertainty; indeed I have never myself discovered which syllables Milton considered short and which long, so as to be able to draw any line between them.

(or shortened) vowel pure, or a short vowel followed by only one consonant. But the rules of stress make a very wide distinction between the heavy long syllables on the one hand, which practically retard speech (whether by virtue of the length of the vowel, as in *brōad*, *brīght*, *dōwn* ; or by a crowding of consonants as in *incēnsebreathing*) ; and those lighter long syllables on the other hand, in which a short vowel, though classically long by position, is not much retarded by consonants (as in *and*, or the second syllable of *brightest*). Stressed verse does not, for instance, make much distinction between the second syllables of *brighter* and *brightest*, though the one would in classical prosody be short, and the other long. Keeping therefore the term *short*, as it is used in the prosody of the Greeks, for the very shortest syllables, it is necessary to make two classes of their *long* syllables ; and these I shall distinguish into *heavy* and *light*, as just explained. And as there will be, in what I shall have to say, seldom any cause to distinguish between the *light* and the *short*, the class *light* will include the short, unless the latter are specially distinguished, and thus it comes about that in stressed verse syllables are primarily classed as *heavy* and *light* instead of *long* and *short*.

accentual heavy and light.

The symbols will therefore be as follows :

symbols defined.

^ denotes a stressed syllable whether light or heavy.

– denotes a heavy syllable as defined.

◡ a light syllable as defined, and will include the short syllables, which may however be sometimes denoted by the lesser short sign .

It is perhaps well to repeat the warning, that as syllables vary in all degrees of quantity from longest to shortest, there cannot be an accurate line drawn between *heavy* and *light* ; and a syllable of intermediate quantity may in some collocations appear heavy, in others light[1]. The typical heavy syllables, however, are always heavy and long, and the typical light syllables are plainly distinguishable from them ; while the true short syllables proper remain always, as in Greek or Latin, an accurately separate class.

The first two rules of stress-prosody which have already been given, are *ex hypothesi.*

The first and second rules.

I. THE STRESS GOVERNS THE RHYTHM.

II. The second rule is a logical corollary from the first, namely, that THE STRESSES MUST ALL BE TRUE SPEECH-STRESSES : i.e. the rhythm must never rely upon the metrical form to supply a stress which not being in the natural speech-intonation, is introduced only by the necessities of the metre. (This is explained on p. 88 ; examples will be found below, exx. 12, 13, 20, 21, 22.) The reader to whom this offers any difficulty should master it at once. The reason for the rule is that since it is the stress that determines the rhythm, the rhythm cannot create the stress. The result of not observing this rule is confusion and uncertainty in the verse : for the ear being called on in any one place to impose a stress which does not exist in the natural reading of the sense, will feel at liberty in other places to refuse the rhythm offered to it ; and will often instinctively replace it by some commoner form, obtained by substituting a metrical false stress, as it has been before compelled to do.

If we now examine any simple verses written on the accentual system, further laws should appear. And since the verse is framed on the stresses, the first

[1] If the reader asks for an example, I suggest the word *young* in ex. 5. *Young* is classically short before a vowel, for this *ng* is only a modified *n*, and the *ou* is of course only the English modified short *a*, which we write *u* ; but being a monosyllable and here before a consonant and in a specially weak place of the line, the syllable seems more heavy than light.

question will be concerning the complements of these stresses: what do these stresses carry with them? Any example will show; the more familiar the better. Bp. Heber's hymn will be well known to most readers.

Complement of stresses.

(1) Brightest and best of the sons of the morning.

This line was no doubt intended by its author for an accentual dactylic line, and would have been scanned by him thus:

Bríghtĕst ănd | bést ŏf thĕ | sóns ŏf thĕ | mórnĭng.

But that is not its right division into stress-units or feet.

III. It is a general law of stress, as I think any one who consults his ear must perceive, that A STRESS HAS MORE CARRYING POWER OVER THE SYLLABLE NEXT TO IT, THAN IT HAS OVER A SYLLABLE REMOVED FROM IT BY AN INTERVENING SYLLABLE. And this rule, supposing it to be the only rule, would give us the following units:

Third rule.

Brîghtĕst | ănd bêst ŏf | thĕ sôns ŏf | thĕ môrnĭng,

which is a better explanation of the verse upon the theory of stress. But this clearly is not right, and a little consideration will convince us of another rule, namely:

IV. That a STRESS HAS A PECULIARLY STRONG ATTRACTION TOWARDS VERBAL UNITY AND FOR ITS OWN PROCLITICS AND ENCLITICS and that it will attach such syllables by preference, and override rule III, unless forbidden by some other law, as it sometimes is by rule V.

Fourth rule.

This law will give the following division:

Brîghtĕst | ănd bêst | ŏf thĕ sôns | ŏf thĕ môrnĭng,

and this is the right explanation of this verse.

I do not see that there is any cause for surprise at finding the metrical units sometimes determined by

Grammar bond.

grammar. The conditions are these: the main element and determinant of the metre is the stress—this is conceded—and this stress is often determined by the grammar. Now the syllables which fall between the stresses must be related to them, and their natural relation is that they depend on them, some on one stress and some on another; and if we question which depend on which, there is no escape from the grammatical speechbond: even the expression of the grammatical stress by musical pitch, is pitch in relation to the parts of the grammatical unit within itself. The only objection which I can imagine is this: an objector may say—'It is true that the stresses do carry the syllables as you explain, but *in doing this they make a dactylic or anapaestic system*; and it is that which satisfies the ear, for the ear is attending to these regular metrical units and not to the irregular speech-units of the stress.' Now I do not at all quarrel with this view. I agree with it so far as to say that, *in proportion as the diction is poetic and the versification good*, regular *metrical units will assert themselves independently of the grammar*, so as to override the irregular units of the speech-stress, and may even come to be the simplest description of some regular accentual English verse. But this is not its true analysis; and I am convinced that if any one who hankers after classical analogies will provisionally cast his fancy aside, and examine the real English construction of the verse, he will never, after understanding it, wish to superimpose upon it a foreign and needless explanation. For the stressed rhythm is a sufficient account of itself: its analysis is complete, and if it is not altogether more beautiful, it is more variously beautiful than any other. I would even say that the analogy with Greek or Latin verse is confusing and worse than useless. Analysis of the English accentual hexameter, for instance, reveals that trochees (so-called) serve for

Grammatical feet *versus* equal or regular metrical units.

spondees, and it is really provoking that any one should persist in pretending to understand an explanation which, basing itself on the distinction between long and short syllables,[1] is reduced to admit that a short syllable will serve for a long one. Besides this absurdity, the analysis of classical verse into classical units is sometimes an arbitrary or doubtful matter when it is at home. The following succession of syllables might, apart from context, be either dactylic or anapaestic.

metrical units often ambiguous.

–◡◡–◡◡–◡◡–

and if it can be either, why may it not equally well be this ?—

–◡|◡–◡|◡–◡|◡–

Certainly classical prosody does not make the slightest *a priori* probability in favour of an anapaestic or dactylic system in English rather than the one last shown. But if the stress-laws be allowed and observed, it matters not what explanation of this sort be indulged in ; and if it can add to the pleasure which any one takes in reading the verse, it is so far good, even though its expositors may not always be able to agree about it among themselves.

The next line will give us more laws. To write it first as the Bishop would have divided it,

Fifth rule.

(2) Dáwn ŏn ōur | dárknĕss ănd | lénd ŭs thīne | áid.

Here are plainly two bad false quantities. *Dawn on our*, and *lend us thine* are very bad even for accentual dactyls. One has only to speak them detached to perceive this. But as they lie in the verse their faultiness does not appear. The line is quite smooth and satisfactory ; it does not halt. How is this ? The reason is that, though a bad accentual dactylic

[1] The long and short syllables of the classical metre being represented by accented and unaccented syllables respectively.

verse, it is a very good line on the principles of stress, dividing thus :

Dawn on | our darkness | and lend us | thine aid.

V. The law which this verse may illustrate is this, that (at least in these light rhythms) A STRESS WILL NOT CARRY A HEAVY SYLLABLE WHICH IS REMOVED FROM IT BY ANOTHER SYLLABLE ; or thus, A HEAVY SYLLABLE MUST BE CONTIGUOUS WITH THE STRESSED SYLLABLE THAT CARRIES IT ; and it will follow from this, that when the first of two proclitics is heavy, the stress will refuse it unless the two can be contracted by speech into one heavy syllable.

Shelley's practice.

There are numberless instances of infraction of this rule in almost all stressed verse hitherto written. Here are some examples from Shelley's *Sensitive Plant*:

(3) *Each and all* like ministering angels were.
(4) *Whilst the lag*ging hours of the day went by.
(5) *Like young lo*vers whom youth and love make dear.
(6) *Wrapped and filled* by their mutual atmosphere.

The reader should consider whether he likes the italicized initial feet of these lines or not ; they have, of course, a definite character of their own, which need not be condemned as bad or intolerable in itself. The question is whether such feet are admissible as units of this light verse. If they are not, then their admission puts the verse into another category, and we must describe it differently : only, since by far the greater part of the poem is in the lighter rhythm, we are in a dilemma ; nor can one be expected to defend a confusion of two kinds of verse. I should certainly rule them out. There is some explanation of Shelley's practice given below, p. 98, with further examples and strictures.

From rule III above, it would appear that so-called

dactyls and *anapaests* must be comparatively rare units in stressed verse, and that the typical trisyllabic foot will be one in which the stress is in the middle, with an unstressed syllable on either side of it, (as I indicated in my earlier edition by placing it first in my list of accentual units) like the word *symmetric*, or *britannic*, which may provisionally be used as a name for these feet.

Table of accentual units

We may now give a list of the common stress-units or feet, which are found in the kind of verse which we are describing.

1st. The bare stress ∧ without any complement. This is frequently found. (An ex. occurs on p. 89.)

2nd. The two falling disyllabic feet:

∧∪
∧–

3rd. The two rising disyllabic feet:

∪∧
–∧

4th. The britannics, or mid-stress trisyllabics:

∪∧∪
–∧∪
∪∧–
–∧–

5th. The so-called dactyl and anapaest, i.e. the falling and rising trisyllabics:

∧∪∪
∪∪∧

6th. The quadrisyllabics:

∪∧∪∪
–∧∪∪
∪∪∧∪
∪∪∧–

7th. The five-syllable foot:

∪∪∧∪∪

which will rarely occur in the rhythms which we are discussing.

excludes one

It will be seen that in the above list there is no example of a heavy and light syllable occurring both on the same side of a stress. The forms –∪∧ and ∧∪–

which Shelley admits.

have been excluded by rule V. The other possible forms are ⏑–∧ and ∧–⏑: of these the second is, I think, rare, and we must be contented here to rule it out by default; of the first, I will give examples from *The Sensitive Plant*, beginning with a full stanza to show the metre.

his practice

And the spríng arosé on the gárden faír,
And the spírit of lóve fell éverywhére;
(7) *Ánd each flówer* and hérb on Eárth's dark bréast
Róse from the dreám of its wíntry rést.
(8) *Ánd their bréath* was míxed with faint ódour sént.
(9) *Ánd narcís*si the faírest amóng them áll.
(10) *Whích unveíled* the dépth of her glówing bréast.
(11) *Cán first lúll* but at lást must awáken ít.

Now if we do not approve of the heaviness of the initial feet italicized in these lines, which plainly I do not, we have to ask why Shelley wrote them. Why did he like them? I think the answer is this. Having chosen this particular metre to write in, that is a stressed rhythm, with liberty to use trisyllabic or disyllabic units at will (a metre sometimes called comic-iambic stanza), he knew that it would play havoc with the gentle mood of his poem if it were not freely broken or delayed; and having no system to govern his liberties in breaking the rhythm, he did just what came most naturally to the language, and overloaded the stresses. And he not only overloaded the stresses, but he did not even keep the stresses intact. The poem is in the same condition as *Christabel* (examined on pp. 87, 88). Here are some of Shelley's false stresses:

his infraction of rule II.

(12) And the Naíad-like líly *óf* the vále.
(13) Till the fíery sún which *ís* its éye.

Weak places, like these third feet, cannot be

admitted in stress-prosody (see rule II, and for the possible omission of stress in stressed verse, p. 105); so that from these and many other lines in the poem it is clear that *The Sensitive Plant* is not written in pure stressed verse, and that Shelley had not, any more than Coleridge, a consistent practice in that system of versification. This is the account of these verses. A consistent prosody is, however, so insignificant a part in what makes good English poetry, that I find that I do not myself care very much whether some good poetry be consistent in its versification or not: indeed I think I have liked some verses better because they do not scan, and thus displease pedants. I should have put Blake into the 'Golden Treasury' in 1861. However, when one is considering prosody and principles of rhythm, it is necessary to attend to that only; and I cannot admit that these verses are good as mere versification. Shelley's practice has naturally done much to accustom our ear to allow these heavy initial feet in light measures; and it has encouraged others to be careless about such syllables, especially as it requires some pains to avoid them. But it should be noted that, in this so-called comic-iambic stanza, the first place is the one to which even the light rising trisyllable is most sparingly admitted by those who have done best in this metre, and *a fortiori*, the heavy rising trisyllables would be excluded entirely.

common in English poets.

Special condition of first foot.

It will be seen that in this metre (in which the lines are very strong, distinct units), this peculiar behaviour of the initial stress of the line in disliking to carry more than one unstressed syllable before it, follows logically from law III above, and confirms the statement that a 'britannic' is the commonest trisyllabic unit of stressed verse. Adopting the classical terminology, the rule would be that in these comic-iambics an anapaest is allowed in any place, but is best excluded from the first. The laws of stress give a perfect account of this, for the first foot is in an exceptional condition, the unstressed syllables that precede its stress having a stress *on one side of them only*; whereas the two unstressed syllables of all the other anapaests have a stress on both sides of them, so that they can divide and go one to one stress and one to another, as they will do if either of them is heavy: and as this is not possible in the first foot, it is for this reason exceptional.

Heine's practice.

Heine's strictness in this respect is one great cause of the crispness and force of this measure in his hands. I cannot do better than give an example of a few stanzas by that master, as they will not only illustrate this point, but will exhibit, better than any words of mine can, the great variety of rhythm possible in the simplest form of strict writing in stress-prosody.

Es tréibt | mich hín, | es tréibt | mich hér!
Noch wénige | Stúnden, | dann sóll ich | sie scháuen,
Sie sélber, | die schőnste | der schőnen | Jungfráuen;—
Du tréues | Hérz, | was póchst du | so schwér!

Die Stúnden | sind áber | ein fáules | Vólk!
Schléppen | sích | beháglich | tráge,
Schléichen | gähnend | íhre | Wége;
Túmmle | dích, | du faúles | Vólk!

Tóbende | Eíle | mich tréibend | erfásst!
Áber | wohl níemals | líebten | die Hóren;—
Héimlich | im gráusamen | Búnde | verschwóren,
Spótten sie | tűckisch | der Líebenden | Hást.

If all these feet, in which more than one heavy syllable is carried by a stress on the same side of it, be ruled out, then the simple general rule would seem to be that—

sixth rule.

VI. A STRESS WILL NOT CARRY MORE THAN ONE HEAVY SYLLABLE OR TWO LIGHT SYLLABLES ON THE SAME SIDE OF IT; and this would be so very like 'Equivalence', that we may join hands with the classicists. I believe that in the lighter trisyllabic rhythms this should be made the rule, and that its infractions should appear as exceptions.

Difficulties. Uncertainty (1) of syllabic length.

The difficulties in the application of such a rule are these: First, the uncertain and even varying length of some of these syllables, and the fact that we are accustomed to hear them contracted or indistinctly pronounced in common talk. Many syllables which would appear to be truly *heavy* if spoken with the full articulation which poetic diction and dignity demand, are as truly *light* in common speech; from which it would follow that the standard of *light* and *heavy* is different in the higher and lower standards of poetic diction and feeling, and that a writer who is lax with his 'quantities' must thereby lower his style: and this is apparent in most examples of accentual verse as it is now written.

(2) of grammatical bond.

Secondly, a very difficult question arises, which affects equally all those units where the stress is apparently overladen on one side or other, and concerning which I do not find it possible to make a clear definition: it is this, how far the refusal of a stress to carry the whole of its grammatical unit (see exx. 22, 25, 26) will cause the thrown-off syllable or syllables to attach themselves to another stress: or, in other words, how far the stresses may be relied on to carry their proper metrical complements *independently of the grammar*. I believe the answer to be that this again depends on the style in which the verse is written; and while in common colloquial language (such as is the greater part of Clough's comic poems) the grammatical bond will assert itself very strongly, yet in a higher poetic diction (even such as Shelley's *Sensitive Plant*) it will readily give way to the claim of the versification. If this is true, then where the grammar is most stringent, there the liberty of treating these heavier syllables freely by contraction and hastening is greatest; while just in those cases where they cannot be hurried and obscured without disgracing the style, the questionable syllables may be resolved into other stresses.

(3) of length of stress.

Thirdly, a question is likely to arise as to the length of the stress. On this point I shall substitute what I have come to think, for what I wrote twenty years ago.

A trained ear is readily sensitive to the length of a stressed syllable, the 'quantity' of an accented syllable being much more undisguisable and exacting than the quantity or length of an unaccented syllable. In practice therefore a versification which always used *long* stresses, would differ from verse that admitted *short* stresses—and it should be noted that in this matter *short* is to be distinguished from *light*: Short stresses occur in the quotation from Shelley on p. 96 in the words *ministering*, *lagging*, and *lovers*. It is doubtful if English readers now distinguish them, but Dr. Henry Bradley tells me that in Anglo-Saxon accentual verse, length was considered a necessary quality of stress; so that if a stress fell on a short syllable, it required another short syllable with it to complete its time, and that the two together were considered as filling the stress place, which was normally occupied by one long syllable. That this is altogether satisfactory to the ear, is shown in the examples from Milton on p. 16, by which I have illustrated it.

Accentual verse therefore, which had only long stresses, could consistently use short syllables in the stress places by aid of this device, and would yet maintain its difference of fluency from verse which admitted a single short syllable as a full stress—and the rule for the longer-stressed verse would be that a short-stressed syllable must always be accompanied by another short syllable to supply its deficiency. But since bare stresses on heavy syllables are doubtless agreeable in all accentual verse, it follows that two short syllables, the first of them accented, might occur as a full unit in either system.

In the stress versification which admitted only long stresses, my symbol ∧ would mean either –́ or ◡́◡, but never ◡́.

(4) of elisions.

Fourthly, it must be decided as to how far the fiction of *elision* is to be allowed. Such a line as

(14) Only' overhead the sweet nightingale

is by our rules good or bad according as the elision is allowed or not. It pleases me.

The main difficulty however lies undoubtedly in the uncertain length of these light longs, and the indisposition of English writers, either to oppose their tendency to intrude, or to allow them their true length; for it is owing to this leniency towards them that so little of our stressed verse is satisfactory to read, or possible to refer to as a mode · one can only wish that the practice were stricter.

§ *Heavier accentual rhythms.*

Double stress

Finally, there is no doubt that this stress-prosody is fit for much heavier rhythms than those which we are considering; and that in such heavier rhythms heavier units or feet would be allowed, though, as these come in, secondary or subordinate accents will appear. A study of Shelley's very beautiful early poem, 'Away, the moor is dark beneath the moon,' will illustrate what I mean. The scheme, on which this poem is written, is one of four main or double stresses in the line; but, if read with due gravity, it will show generally six accents, and sometimes five or seven. Shelley was of course conscious that the various stress-rhythms with which he was, so to speak,

example in Shelley

counterpointing the original measure, were destructive of its singsong framework: for instance

(15) Rapid | clouds | have drunk | the last | pale beam | of even

is convincing and extremely fine, whereas

Rapid clouds have drunk | the last pale beam of even

is altogether unworthy; and so of most of the lines.

The scheme of the first line, which looks like a common syllabic 'iambic' line, of five feet, is this:

(16) Away, the moor | is dark beneath the moon.

A musical time beat

And any one who would read this poem aloud, or the one next mentioned, must be acquainted with the skeleton scheme of four double stresses and the break in the midline, and give indication of these, as may be done by keeping just in touch with the musical time-accent; the musical scheme being what used to be called *Alla breve*, that is with four minims to a bar, with some secondary accent on the third of them, and liberty to introduce triplets. The variant rhythms which this scheme allows are purposely elaborated towards the end with a great effect of luxuriance; but the two lines here scanned with the double accent will enable any one to scan the rest.

another example of same metre.

This most pathetic poem[1] cannot be made the subject of dry metrical analysis without apology: we shall find however some exculpation, for in seeking another example of Shelley's use of this metre, we come upon the song of the sixth Spirit in the first act of *Prometheus*:

(17) 'Ah, sister, desolation | is a delicate thing.'

[1] My early belief that it recorded the disaster of Shelley's first passion led me to make a futile reflection now corrected.

And it is interesting to discover that Shelley is there recurring to the form which had once spontaneously clothed his own personal emotion.

In such heavier and freer measures (and this rule may be extended to the accentual hexameter) it will be found that the ear will tolerate the omission of a stress under certain conditions. As far as I know, the law is this:

Seventh rule.

VII. IN SOME METRES WHEN FOUR, AND IN ANY METRE WHEN MORE THAN FOUR, UNSTRESSED SYLLABLES OCCUR TOGETHER, THEY WILL OCCUPY THE PLACE OF A STRESS, WHICH MAY BE SAID TO BE DISTRIBUTED OVER THEM; AND A LINE IN WHICH SUCH A COLLECTION OF SYLLABLES OCCURS WILL LACK ONE OF ITS STRESSES.

§ *The accentual hexameter.*

Above accentual rules should govern English accentual hexameter.

If these are the simple primary laws of the lighter (so-called dactylic and anapaestic) forms of stressed verse—and they must be these or something very like them—then they must be the true account of the English 'accentual hexameter'. The rationale of that verse is that it substitutes six stresses or speech-accents, with their complements, for the six quantitive feet of the classic hexameter, and this in spite of the fact that the classic hexameter did not always have six accents: it regards that hexameter as a falling rhythm, and represents the trisyllabic dactyl by two unaccented syllables following their stress, and the spondee by one. Any attempt to supply the falling syllables of the dactyl with short syllables rather than long, or the spondees with long ones rather than short, seems a matter of taste, or a refinement of scholastic fancy.

As this English verse is built on stress, and neglects quantity, it is *absolutely certain* that it must come under the laws of stress and not of quantity. It is plain that quantitive explanation must be absurd; and if our laws of stress-prosody fail to explain it, then we must have laid them down wrongly, and we may test or correct them by it. But if, on the other hand, we find that it is well explained by our laws, we shall not only have a simple and intelligible explanation in lieu of one that is both forced and unintelligible, but shall also establish the truth of our inductions.

Any one who has read, or tried to read,[1] many of these 'hexameters' will remember that, while there are a majority of lines which read fairly well without halting, there are many that are very defective in rhythm; by which I mean that they offer no convincing rhythm to the ear. Among the former class (those that seem to scan) there are some that are extremely fluent, where all the unaccented syllables of the 'dactyls' are light, or even short; and sometimes the falling syllables of the spondees are long. Here is an example:

(18) Tibur is beautiful too, and the orchard slopes and the Anio.

And here is one really accentual, but made to scan on Latin rules:

(19) Out of a dark umbrage sounds also musical issued.

Such verses as these cannot offend any of our laws; all the feet are easily resolved into very simple stress-units. But among those that please there are also

[1] 'Tried to read' is true of most of this verse; and no one can have failed in the trial more thoroughly than I have. My quotations are from Clough because I have found him an exception, and am charmed with the sympathetic spirit of his *Bothie* and *Amours*, in which he has handled aspects of life, the romance of which is very untractable to the Muse, and chosen for them a fairly satisfactory though not a perfected form. If Clough did not quite know what he was doing in the versification (and if he had known, he could have used some of his liberties more freely, and others more sparingly), yet he knew very well what he was not doing.

some which cannot be explained on the hypothesis of (even accentual) dactyl and spondee; and taking these as one class, and those which absolutely refuse to be read as another class, we shall find that the former are pleasing because they are good verses according to stress-prosody; while those which offend are offensive because they break the rules of stressed verse. I will give enough examples to enable any one to apply the test for himself.

its lines offend the ear if they break the rules

The first line of *The Bothie* is a halting line:

(20) Ìt was the áfternóon and the spórts were nów at the énding.

This offends against rule II. There is a metrical accent in the first place (on *it*) instead of a speech-accent, and the verse will not read without distorting the intonation. The same fault occurs in the following verse:

(21) Ànd she got | úp from her | séat on the | róck putting | bý her | knítting.

But if the accent be put on its proper place (on *got* instead of on *and*), the verse, though not praiseworthy, will read, and scan in stress-prosody.

And she got | up | from her seat | on the rock | putting by | her knitting.

Compare the final metrical units as differently explained by the two prosodies.

So I find in Longfellow's *Evangeline*:

(22) Ànd they rode | slówly a|lóng through the | wóods con|ver-sing to|géther.

This halting line offends law II in the first foot, and law IV in his third. If the grammar happened to require a stress on *they*, the first place would be cured:

And they | rode slowly | along | through the wood | con-versing | together.

but please if they keep them

But the heavy syllable *through* belongs to *wood*, and, if read with that stress, will make the place halt; whereas it refuses to be attached to *along*.

In order to exhibit plainly that the reason why this line halts in that place is not because there is a heavy syllable where there may not be one, but only that it is collocated by grammar with a wrong stress (as ruled by law V), compare the following line (again Longfellow), where the third place is identical in quantity; and yet the verse reads well:

(23) Só is it | bést, Jóhn | Éstaugh, we | wíll not | spéak of it | fúrther.

however the quantitive rules are transgressed.

And observe that it reads well because the heavy syllable *taugh* is attached to its contiguous stress.

So is | it best, | John Estaugh, | we will not | speak of it | further.

The following verse from Clough reads quite well:

(24) Yea and | shall hodmen | in beershops | complain | of a glory | denied them.

But consider *beershopscompl* as a dactyl!

The following verse also scans in spite of a bad dactyl in the second place:

(25) Yés and I | féel the life|juíces of | áll the | wórld and the | áges.

because its units will divide thus:

Yes and | I feel the | lifejuices | of all | the world and | the ages.

Example of grammatical bond broken.

Lifejuices does not refuse to part with its article; and I think this line will serve for an example of how a little poetic diction will relax a grammatical bond (as explained above, p. 101). The reason of this probably is that 'Lifejuices' as a verbal unit is so rich in significance as to distract and absorb the attention wholly to itself, and it does this by means of the changed voice-tone that it evokes, which cannot be anticipated and shared by its article. The following line, which is in much the same metrical condition, halts because the diction is *guindée*, and the grammar-bond fast:

(26) Nóble ládies their prízes adjúdged fŏr cōstúme that was pérfect.

The two explanations contrasted.

The word *for* will not leave *costume*, the stress of which is already fully occupied.

The following pleasant line,—

(27) Bright October was come, the misty, bright October.

would be thus scanned on the classical system:

Bríght Oc|tóber was | cóme, the | místy, | bríght Oc|tóber.

Whereas, on the stress system it is thus:

Brîght | Ōctôbĕr | wăs côme, | thĕ mîstў, | brîght | Ōctôbĕr.

The following is a line which Clough would never have written, had he imagined himself to be making classical hexameters:

(28) With a mathematical score hangs out at Inverary.

This is of course irreducible to classic feet, but the verse reads well enough because it does not offend the laws of stressed verse; though I do not know what is the correct division of *Inverary*:

Wĭth ă mâ|thēmâtĭcăl | scôre | hāngs ôut | ăt În|vĕrâră.

This may lead to the remark that words of four or more syllables, which have two speech-stresses in them, are generally in this condition; though it is impossible that they should ever give rise to any difficulty or uncertainty of rhythm, they often refuse to be divided, or, which is the same thing, offer two equally satisfactory alternatives.

It appears from verses like the last that there is no objection to the occurrence of an unstressed syllable (or even of two short syllables) before the first stress of the line in these accentual hexameters, as some writers have perceived, and trusting to their ear have used it. It is of course quite out of order in classical prosody, and it dispels the last remnant of illusion.

Very soon after writing the above examination of accentual English verse I came into possession of Professor Skeat's great edition of Chaucer; and I found that he analyses English syllabic verse into the very same speech-units which I had attributed to the modern accentual verse, and his list of stress-units corresponds with that on p. 72 of my old book. (See note L.)

I do not wish to criticise any of his details, but his teaching compels me to explain that I do not think it justifiable to base the structure of Chaucer's verse on an accentual system: he seems to me to be confusing rhythm with prosody. No doubt all verse derives its beauty mainly from its speech-rhythms, but these are not the prosody, they are the rhythms which are allowed and ordered by the prosody.

This much will be plain to all classical scholars: they know that their verses must scan; and when they learn to write quantitive verse they are not taught Greek and Latin rhythms, but the prosodial laws of long and short syllables, of feet, cæsuras, elisions and so forth, that is to say the prosody; and when they know these they can write what rhythms please them or may chance to come, and they may be content in their Latin hexameters with the praise that they have well imitated Virgil's rhythms.

That seems a very clear distinction; and just as quantitive verse has its quantitive prosody, so syllabic verse has its syllabic prosody, and accentual verse will have its accentual prosody. All three are equally dealing with speech-rhythm, and they all approach it differently, and thus obtain different effects. It might be possible perhaps, as it is certainly conceivable, to base the whole art of versification on speech-rhythm, and differentiate the prosodies secondarily by their various qualities of effect upon the speech. But no one has ever attempted that.

The fact that rhythm is so much more evident than prosody, and is felt to lie so much nearer to the poetic effects, inclines people to think that prosody is pedantic rubbish, which can only hamper the natural expression of free thought and so on. But in all arts the part that can be taught is the dry detail of the material which has to be conquered; and it is no honour to an art to despise its grammar.

If any one should refuse to make the distinction which I have drawn between syllabic and accentual verse and think to overset it by replying that all verse is both syllabic and accentual, I would offer him the following considerations :—

When reading Milton's or Chaucer's ten-syllable verse aloud, the occurrence of a line deficient in one of the ten syllables (and such lines occur in Chaucer) proves extremely awkward both for hearer and reader, especially if the reader is unprepared for it. It cannot escape observation : and if a line occurs in which there are more than ten syllables, the 'trisyllabic foot' is readily perceived ; so that of every line, as it is read, the hearer can say at once of how many syllables it was composed, whether of nine, ten, eleven or twelve. But he will not observe a variety in the number of stresses in the same way ; whether the line have its full complement of five, or only four (as is very frequent), or only three, no awkwardness or interruption of rhythm will be perceived ; nor will the hearer be able to say readily at the close of any line how many true stresses it contained. This is syllabic verse.

Of stressed verse exactly the contrary is true. The omission of an initial unaccented syllable from the line produces no awkwardness: hearer and reader alike are indifferent as to the number of syllables which go to make the line; nor, as each line is read, can they say how many syllables have gone to make it. But if a stress be omitted, they perceive the rhythm to be unsatisfactory, and readily detect the awkwardness of the false metrical stresses which they passed over in the syllabic verse. This is stressed or accentual verse.

And the quantitive system shows the very same distinction; for in reading Virgil the frequently occurring line of five accents is regular in metre and rhythm, whereas in the English accentual hexameter it does not scan.

NOTES

Note A. to preface.

The history of this book must supply the apology which it has long needed, whether or no it may deserve it.

Thirty-three years ago the late Dean of Norwich, who was then rector of the church where I was precentor, undertook for the Clarendon Press to edit the first book of *Paradise Lost* as a school text. He besought me to contribute such an account of the versification as should knock out the prevalent usage of misreading the rhythm; for it was generally thought necessary and correct to mispronounce words so as to make them scan with regular alternate accent. I consented, and adapting my method to my audience was fortunate enough to be immediately convincing. This success induced the Delegates of the Press to issue my notes as a separate treatise, which converted some young poets, who 'nimbly began dancing'; and they introduced Miltonic inversions so freely into their blank verse that champions of the prevailing orthodoxy raised an indignant protest in the newspapers, wherein the discussion grew so incredibly hot that a London evening journal advertised 'prosody' as an attractive item in its daily posters. From that day the book has been on a false footing, and to me a perennial discomfort, as in succeeding editions I laboured to make it worthier of its wider public. Incidentally I came to learn more about the subject than I understood when I began with it; and I have therefore welcomed the invitation which the publishers made me last year that I would finally rehandle it. In this revision, though I could not look to excel in a business so desperately alien to my natural faculties and inclination, and was indeed disheartened by the frequent misinterpretations that I had brought on myself, yet I have spared no patience in trying to render my original remarks more intelligible, and to methodize my stray notes; and I trust that the headlines and marginal analysis will sufficiently exhibit the construction of the book, and even in the absence of any index make detailed reference easy; so that I may after all perhaps succeed in winning some pardon for the annoyance which I have so often conveyed with my opinions to the readers of its predecessors.

I have attempted also to set the facts on their proper phonetic basis, but am well aware that good intentions cannot make up for lack of early training in phonetics; it is a subject which needs a young ear, and my late adventures in that field can only modestly claim to be of use to those who being in a like stage of learning with myself may possibly listen more readily to a learner than to an expert. I wish that the book may do something to conquer the prejudice which still opposes reform of this fundamental defect in our early education. If I could have my school-life over again, my most earnest supplication would be that I should be taught language by men who knew the alphabet. For an alphabet is a phonetic device, and my teachers did not know their A B C. The sole reason why Englishmen are commonly such bad linguists is that their own language is written so unphonetically that the alphabet does not serve its essential purpose; it is rather the cause of an immediate blank confusion of mind. My first encounter with it in the nursery was to hear that C A T (see, ey, tee) spelt *cat*, whereas it spells *sate*; and that D O G (dee, owe, gee) spelt *dog*, whereas it spells *doge*: and there are very few of my contemporaries who will listen to common sense in this matter, or allow the clear light of scientific method to dispel the mystifications which prevent our children from understanding the elements of speech. And the further they proceed in the higher education the more hopelessly are they involved and confirmed in their ignorance: the barbarous distortion of Latin in our great schools is strenuously upheld as a reasonable propriety which it is almost a national offence to discredit; and I found the other day that I had hurt a scholar's feelings when I laughed at the pronunciation VEE in VAE VICTIS, and remarked that that was a most unnatural and inept exclamation for the expression of extreme woe, and seemed to hail from Dante's limbo of the unbaptized

> ove i lamenti
> Non suonan come GUAI, ma son sospiri:

the Latin word being actually identical with the Greek οὐαι, with which the Greek testament has made us all familiar.

> 'And now it wounds whom it astounds
> To hear that speech is made of sounds,
> Phonetical—(O word of fear
> Unpleasing in a marrèd ear).'

NOTE B. to p. 6.

The allowance of the final extrametrical syllable in English decasyllabic verse requires no explanation or defence; it is well, however, to note that Milton was sparing in its use in spite of the rhythmical example and influence of Dante's hendecasyllabic lines. But when Milton applies his full liberty of accentual inversion to his lyrical verse in the choruses of *Samson Agonistes*, it appears to me an anomaly, an illogical complication without advantage and even a hindrance to the free development of the scheme; so as it would seem that his next step might have been to disallow it in the lyrical verse.

When with this conviction I made myself the experiment of excluding it, the consistency resulted in quite unexpected and novel effects of rhythm, which can be observed and judged of in four poems printed in my last book (*October*, *etc.*, Heinemann, 1920), where the metre is explained in a note as being, for good or ill, merely a logical development of Milton's syllabic rules.

Note C. to p. 24. Tiresias.

And Tiresias and Phineus Prophets old. *P. L.* iii. 36.

This line troubles some readers, but it is not an irregular verse. The elision (synalœpha) is in the last two vowels of Tiresias. The line is sufficient evidence that Milton accented the second syllable of Tiresias, and pronounced the first long. It does not in itself decide the quality of the *e*, but it would seem that Milton may have pronounced it short, as it is in Greek and Latin verse.

There is the same inversion of accent in the second foot, and the same synalœpha as Dante uses with the similar name Virgilio, which he similarly places after a monosyllable at the beginning of the line:

E Virgilio rispose: Voi credete. *Purg.* ii, t. 21.
Pur Virgilio si trasse a lei, pregando. vi, t. 13.
O Virgilio, Virgilio, chi è questa? xix, t. 10.

Nor is this any unusual licence, for we find 'Del retaggio' and 'In opprobrio', &c., beginning lines.

There can be little doubt that Milton's admiration of Dante's rich rhythms was the main cause of his own: and that he sought to improve our English verse by the same accentual variety. I have made no comparative count of the inversions in Dante and Milton, but I am conversant with Dante's rhythms, and should expect statistics to show that one main difference lay in the greater frequency of inversion of the fourth foot in Dante. The effect of this inversion constitutes in the *Commedia* a typical form of the metre, no doubt invited by the unbroken regular accentuation of the trisyllabic last foot, which called for neighbourly alleviation, just as the accentual endings which the Latin language enforced on Virgil's hexameter made the inverted feet at the beginning of his line more desirable.

The objection to the Tiresias line in Milton arises solely from prejudice in readers' ears against inversion of the second foot. But this irregularity is an intentional effect and should be welcome in its place. Familiarity with Dante's poem should quickly correct their taste. Let them study the rhythm of this masterly passage from the first Canto of the Purgatory (I accent the inversions):

Chi vi fu lucerna,
Uscendo fuor déllа profonda notte,
Che sempre nera fa la valle inferna?
Són le léggi d'Abisso così rotte?
O è mutato in ciel nuóvo consiglio
Che, dannáti, venite álle mie grotte?—
Lo duca mio allor mi diè di piglio,
E con parole e con máni e con cenni
Reverénti mi fe' le gambe e 'l ciglio.
Póscia rispose a lui—Da me non venni,
Dónna scése del ciel, &c. . . .

Note D. to p. 37. 'stand alone.'

But if the practically impossible synalœpha of 'the harp' printed on p. 26 be disallowed, that verse gives the contraction of 'to the': and there is no doubt that the line will be rhythmically read by virtue of that contraction rather than by the fictive elision.

Note E. to p. 49. 'I shall show later.'

The passage which kept this promise having been exscissored must be restored here:

'It may at first seem childish to assert that "something extraordinary" in the sense determined "something extraordinary" in the prosody; yet to deny this requires the acceptance of an unlikely alternative: we must believe that at the crisis in the poem, where Samson declares that he feels within him the divine impulse which leads to the catastrophe of the tragedy, there occurs by accident a violent rhythmical jar in the verse.'

And surely this is exactly what an actor would ask for: he would have to make up something arresting in the speech if it were not supplied to him.

Note F. p. 49, *at foot.*

A sustained formal dignity of diction is essential to the command of style, and it closely affects the prosody of verse, as appears in the remarks on the varying length of syllables and on the grammatical speech-bond in accentual verse (p. 101), and the illustration of it in the last quotation on p. 105. Any careless sinking from it kills the meaning and effect of its gradations where the diction is sensitively following the gradations of dignity in the subject-matter; and this is an irreparable dead loss. Thus, for example, the omission of the relative pronoun is a conversational licence, but is now commonly employed by all writers, even where it causes grammatical ambiguity: I suppose there will be no instance of it in *Paradise Lost* until Adam and Eve, having fallen, fall to mutual recrimination. Its sudden intrusion, therefore, has its full force, when 'from distempered breast Adam, estranged in look and altered style', says:

> Let none henceforth seek needless cause to approve
> The Faith they owe (ix..1141);

its effect is that of emotion being let loose and bursting a bond, and the means will be unobserved: but in calling attention to this detail the word 'style' comes to be absurdly focussed in its self-conscious correctness, and appears near the borderline of pedantry, on one side or the other.

NOTE G. to p. 51.

The poem which I consider to be an actual example of excellence having been unappreciated because the metre was not understood, is Shelley's 'Away! the moor', the metre of which (see p. 104) was explained in my edition of 1901. *The Golden Treasury* published in 1861 did not contain it, and I think that it was not to be found in common anthologies, but that it is now generally received.

NOTE H. to p. 56. 'the poet's intention.'

My own opinion is that this line 'In the camp of Dan' should have been printed with contraction *i'th* or *ith'*, as in some other places. But as the contraction is not printed, I was bound to allow the line to be a possible exception to the general rising rhythm.

NOTE J. to p. 81. Nares's test.

I gave no particular attention to this question of unusual accentuation: and examination shows Nares's list to be inaccurate and misleading. Bradshaw's concordance enables me to tabulate some facts.

The following seventeen words in my list from Nares occur only once each. Brígad, Colleágue, Commércing, Comráde, Consúlt (s), Cóntribute, Convóy (s), Egréss, Midníght (s), Precíncts, Procínct, Prodúct, Reflúx (probably thus, but réflux would scan well), Sepúlchred, Sunshíne (s) (the adjective is always súnshine), Survéy (s), Volúbil (distinguished from figurative vóluble).

Exile (subst.) seems to be exíle. The verb exiled in two places only, and in both might be éxiled with a common inversion. iv. 106, *S. A.* 98.

Process occurs twice and is in same condition as exiled.

Réceptacle. This accentuation is still prevalent, I believe, in Scotland, and lingers among old-fashioned speakers in England.

Sunbéam is printed as two words.

Travérse, verb, in i. 568. It is strange that in the only other place where it occurs this accentuation gives a disagreeable echo. ix. 66.

> From Pole to Pole traversing each Colure;
> On the eighth return'd, and on the Coast averse.

The following four words, Fárewell, Mánkind, Odórous, Sojoúrn, I have deleted from the list. The account of them appears to be thus:

(1) Farewell is much as we say it: a typical illustration is iv. 108–9:

> So farwel Hope, and with Hope farwel Fear,
> Farwel Remorse:

where the third occurrence seems to prefer farewéll, which is the accentuation in *S. A.* 959, 1413.

(2) Mankind. Milton's accentuation seems to have the common liberty: a typical line is viii. 358:

> Above mankinde, or aught then mankinde higher.

(3) Odorous. Milton has ódorous in eight places. Nares asserts odórous presumably on authority of v. 482.

> . . . last the bright consummate floure
> Spirits odorous breathes: flours and thir fruit . . .

but here the unusual accentuation would confirm a suspicion of the text.

(4) Sojourn. The verb is sójourn in xii. 159, and in vii. 249 begins the line. The subst. in *P. R.* iii. 235 is sójourn, and in *P. L.* iii. 15 will thus scan with inversion of third foot:

> In that obscure sojourn, while in my flight.

Note K. to p. 87. 'a skeleton of its own.'

The introduction of true syllabic-verse effects into poems which are otherwise written on an accentual basis is so common now with almost all versifiers that it seems desperate to attempt to convince any one of the impropriety. Every poet is familiar with the old verse, and it is difficult for him to resist ekeing out his lawless and often careless accentual lines with the solid old-fashioned established beauties which he knows will be grateful to his readers. He does not observe that the two different techniques will not sort together: and that if, in the midst of his accentual lines, the old-fashioned syllabic cadences retain any of the effect for which they are valued, it can only be because the quality of the rest of his verse is so indeterminate and unsatisfactory. If his accentual verse had any fixed rule or prosody, then the syllabic verses would offend by breaking those rules. A modern musician knows very well that he cannot obtain the beautiful effects of the ancient vocal counterpoint by interlarding scraps of it into a movement where the discords are unprepared. If such an old-fashioned passage were introduced with any artistic effect, it would owe that effect to contrast, and it would have to be long enough to establish a definite contrast, and that would depend on its incompatibility.

NOTE L. to p. 110. Skeat's analysis of Chaucer's verse.

It is at p. lxxxii of his sixth volume, dated 1894 and issued in the following year. The date of the edition of my tract which contained my original account of stress-units was 1893, and Professor Skeat had read it in manuscript and written many pages of notes upon it. I do not wish to imply that he must consciously or unconsciously have derived his notions from my manuscript; but since my fuller description of accentual verse was not published until eight years after, it might appear in that that I had borrowed from him.

I think that any one who compared his disquisition with mine of 1893 would be struck by the identity of the points that are prominently advanced. He begins with these words: *The structure of English versification has been much obscured by the use of classical terms*; to which point I had devoted my Appendix G, 'on the use of Greek terminology in English prosody' (p. 71 of my old text); and on his next page, *A strong syllable* (that is a strongly-accented syllable) *situated between two weak ones, in such a word as 'alighted', may be called an 'amphibrach'. The amphibrach plays a highly important part in English verse, though it is usual not to mention it at all.* Now these amphibrachs were originally isolated and set first in the list of stress-units on p. 72 of my tract. Again on his page lxxxv, *The poet is so far from conforming to the uniform type of line that he usually does his best to avoid it; and the more skilfully he does this, the more he is appreciated for his variety.* This overstatement of my contention is very strange if set beside Professor Skeat's usual method of scanning Chaucer's verses; indeed the two are irreconcilable. The above quotations and some similar coincidences have provoked me to vindicate the priority of my own work.

PRINTED IN GREAT BRITAIN
AT THE UNIVERSITY PRESS, OXFORD
BY VIVIAN RIDLER
PRINTER TO THE UNIVERSITY